CEDAR GROVE CEMETERY

Portsmouth
Virginia

Plot Book 1 and Book 2

Bettie Jo Matthews

HERITAGE BOOKS
2015

HERITAGE BOOKS
AN IMPRINT OF HERITAGE BOOKS, INC.

Books, CDs, and more—Worldwide

For our listing of thousands of titles see our website
at
www.HeritageBooks.com

Published 2015 by
HERITAGE BOOKS, INC.
Publishing Division
5810 Ruatan Street
Berwyn Heights, Md. 20740

International Standard Book Numbers
Paperbound: 978-1-55613-635-1
Clothbound: 978-0-7884-8621-0

CONTENTS

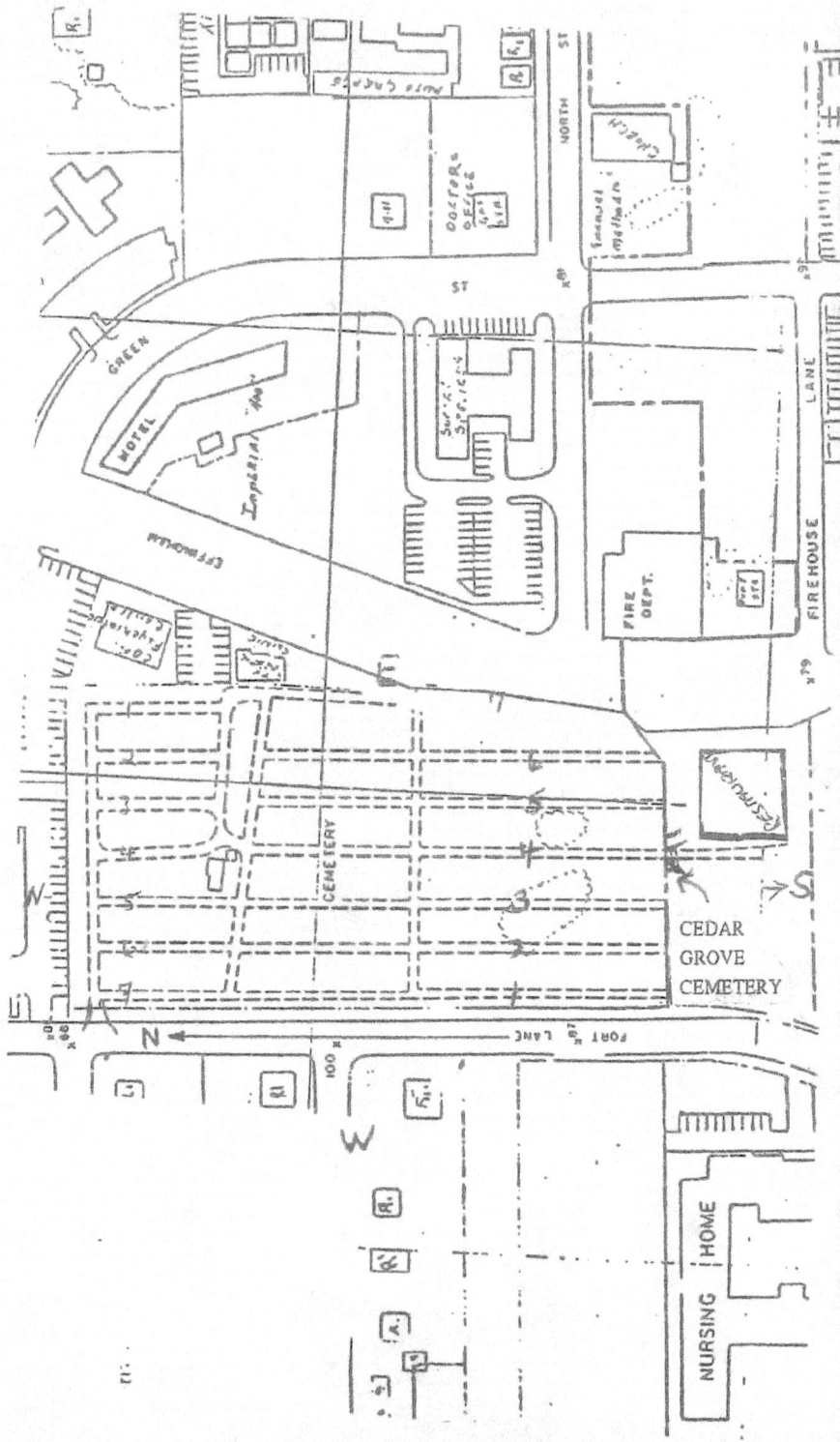

CEDAR
GROVE
CEMETERY

CEMETERY

NURSING HOME

FIRE DEPT.

FIREHOUSE LANE

NORTH ST

DOCTORS OFFICE

ST

GREEN

MOTEL

FORT LANE

INTRODUCTION

The town of Portsmouth was established in 1752 on land owned by Colonel William Craford. He hired a county surveyor, Gershom Nimmo, to divide the sixty-five acres of his plantation into a town to be called Portsmouth, named after a seacoast town in England. Portsmouth was located on the Elizabeth River, the route travel and trade was carried on in that period of time. Portsmouth, a seacoast town, with abundance of the best pine and fir trees in the area, soon became a successful seaport. Trading and shipbuilding brought a need for skilled carpenters, shipwrights, sailmakers, shipbuilders, sea captains.

The Portsmouth town line extended east to west - from Elizabeth River, Water Street, Crawford Street, ending at Middle Street. North to south - from Elizabeth River, North Street, Glasgow Street, London, Queen, High, King, County, Crabbe (later called Columbus) South, and then Bart. The north side of Portsmouth was called "Old Town," and past Bart was the section known as Gosport, later called Newtown. The Newtown section was settled by the Irish and had fallen into such disrepair during the past ten years that it was torn down. Beyond the Gosport section was the Gosport Navy Yard. Since the Civil War, the Navy Yard has been owned by the United States Government and called Norfolk Naval Ship Yard. The Navy Yard extends, along with other government land, all along the Elizabeth River from the old Coast Guard Station to St. Julius Creek. The warehouses and docks that once lined the Elizabeth River at Water Street have been replaced with the Municipal Building. The boardwalk extends the length of Columbia to North Streets with a park at the foot of High Street. The city line in 1832 extended to Chesnut Street.

Until 1832, there were no public places in Portsmouth to bury the dead except various church yards or private plots in gardens. This practice was forbidden in 1832 when the legislature of the state authorized the town trustee of Portsmouth, Virginia, to enforce that there be no burials within the city limits. The first public cemetery was Cedar Grove. The cemetery was purchased in 1833 with the cost for residents to open a grave at $8.00 and $10.00 to nonresidents. The first keeper of Cedar Grove Cemetery was the town sergeant who was paid $50.00 a year. Cedar Grove Cemetery which is a landmark is located west of Effingham Street which, in 1832, was out of the city limits. A group of Portsmouth residents headed by Bill Blake have formed an organization called "Friends of the Cedar Grove Cemetery." This group will see that the cemetery is maintained properly and kept free of vandalism which has occurred in the past.

This book has Cedar Grove Cemetery plot book information with owner and specific location of the burial plot, date of burial, death date, age at death, and relatives of the deceased in some cases. The author has copied complete inscriptions from all the stones in Cedar Grove Cemetery which also includes inscriptions from Trinity Church Yard, the oldest cemetery in Portsmouth. Copies of this information as well as research services are available from the author upon request.

CEDAR GROVE CEMETERY

PLOT BOOK 1

LOT 1
Ave. 8
Owner - Jeff A. Phillips
Infant Phillips - died June 21, 1887, age 5 mos.
Mary Phillips - Oct. 7, 1891, age 5 1/2 mos.
Cecil Phillips - Aug. 7, 1948, age 64 yrs.
Calder S. Phillips - May 25, 1958, age 81 yrs.
Carry Ruth Phillips - Dec. 14, 1934, age 79 yrs.
Arthur J. Phillips - Dec. 17, 1921, age 68 yrs., CSA.
Arthur Jefferson Phillips, Jr. - Aug. 11, 1970 (vault).
Grace Phillips - wife of John Garland Pollard, Gov. of Va., died
    May 4, 1932, age 59 yrs.
Charles T. Phillips - Feb. 15, 1910, age 72 yrs.
Carroll Phillips - Nov. 26, 1943, age 68 yrs.
Kate Shepperd - Dec. 1, 1929, age 71 yrs.

LOT 2
Ave. 8
Owner - John D. Powell, W / H (West Half)
Calder Phillips Williams - Feb. 14, 1920, age 3 days.
Virginia Phillips Powell - Feb. 28, 1920, age 33 yrs.

LOT 3
Ave. 8
Owner - George W. Wrymouth, E / H (East Half)
George W. Wrymouth - Nov. 27, 1889, age 37 yrs.
Kate Hall Phillips Weymouth - Jan. 1929, age 70 yrs.
W. M. W. Weymouth - Apr. 20, 1958, age 75 yrs.
Katherine Phillips Williams - Feb. 13, 1920, age 29 yrs.
Avery Phillips Johnston - Oct. 1, 1961, age 51 yrs.
William Infant - age 3 days.

1

LOT 4

Ave. 8

Owner - F. T. Tynan

Cote - stillborn, Oct. 14, 1913.

Margaret E. Tynan - July 16, 1905, age 34 yrs.

Georgiana Tynan - Nov. 23, 1894, age 47 yrs.

Francis T. Tynan - Nov. 28, 1928, age 89 yrs., CSA and Chief of Police Dept.

John T. Tynan - Feb. 26, 1914, age 38 yrs.

Teresa Tynan - 1874-1875.

Clarence W. Green - Oct. 26, 1907, age 1 yr. and 6 mos.

William V. Tynan - Sept. 27, 1918, age 32 yrs.

Cleara Louise Tynan Cote - Nov. 10, 1913, age 30 yrs.

Blanche T. Tynan - May 13, 1955, age 70 yrs.

Francis C. Tynan - Feb. 3, 1960 (vault).

LOT 5

Ave. 8

Owner - D. W. Ballentine

Mary C. Shannon - Oct. 13, 1953, age 60 yrs.

5 graves - no names (unknown).

Robert Ballentine - Oct. 5, 1895, age 22 yrs. 10 mos.

Linscott Ballentine - May 13, 1914.

Mrs. Ballentine - buried Apr. 27, 1885.

Sarah C. Ballentine - died May 18, 1907, age 48 yrs.

Robert G. Ballentine - June 14, 1922, age 62 yrs.

Leon Garland Shannon - died Aug. 4, 1934, age 56 yrs.

W. L. Shannon - buried Feb. 26, 1894, age 46 yrs.

Eliza Oliver Shannon - died June 21, 1908, age 52 yrs.

LOT 6

Ave. 8

Owner - O. D. Ball

Mrs. Eleanor A. King - Apr. 3, 1885, age 70 yrs.

Helen F. Ball - July 2, 1895, age 46 yrs.

Francis E. Ball - Feb. 4, 1904, age 86 yrs.

Owen Dorsey Ball - Nov. 25, 1898, age 81 yrs.

Mary Henrietta Ball - July 20, 1917, age 66 yrs.

Charles M. Ball - age 20 yrs.

Samuel Boyd Ball - 1857-1932 (cremated).

Lula Blair Ball - 1868-1938 (cremated).

LOT 7

Ave. 8

Owners - E. S. Anderton and James Peterson
Helen M. Anderton - June 10, 1889, age 1 yr. 9 mos.
John W. Anderton - age 10 mos.
Annie Anderton - June 13, 1953, age 93 yrs.
Edward S. Anderton - 1852-1936, age 83 yrs. and 8 mos.
Fannie E. Anderton - buried Nov. 9, 1892, age 64 yrs.
Arlene Peterson - Sept. 8, 1974.
Eliza Jane Peterson - 1853-1914, age 60 yrs.
Jane Peterson - 1847-1912, age 64 yrs.
Augustus E. Peterson - Mar. 5, 1951, age 79 yrs.
Lillian Mae Peterson - Jan. 12, 1962, age 80 yrs.
J. G. Peterson - buried Feb. 6, 1883, age 10 yrs.
Peterson - stillborn, Mar. 30, 1912.

LOT 8
Ave. 8
Owners - J. A. and C. W. Hudgins
Earl P. Hudgins - Feb. 9, 1908, age 1 yr.
Margaret Lorene Hudgins - Feb. 23, 1902, age 1 yr.
Jesse Columbus Hudgins - Jan. 13, 1916, age 10 yrs.
Margaret S. Hudgins - Aug. 29, 1887, age 35 yrs. 8 mos.
C. W. Hudgins - May 24, 1886, age 36 yrs.
Sarah Frances Hudgins - Oct. 25, 1926, age 69 yrs.
Jefferson A. Hudgins - Apr. 1, 1903, age 49 yrs.
Josiah J. Hudgins - Feb. 21, 1889, age 71 yrs.
Mrs. H. Hudgins - Oct. 13, 1884, age 63 yrs.
Margaret Hudgins - Nov. 12, 1910, age 58 yrs.

LOT 9
Ave. 8
Owner - L. C. Godwin
6 graves - no names.
Ida A. Godwin - Jan. 27, 1898, age 50 yrs.
Frances M. Godwin - Feb. 26, 1906, age 54 yrs.
Harry Morserate Godwin - Mar. 7 1885, age 19 yrs.
Teresa Tynan Godwin - Feb. 7, 1928, age 83 yrs.
Leroy Craft Godwin - Sept. 28, 1899, age 62 yrs., CSA.
Genevion Godwin - Dec. 6, 1940, age 62 yrs.
Henry B. Godwin - (reinterred from 44) Apr. 30, 1890.
Sarah F. Godwin - Apr. 13, 1892, age 47 yrs.
Virginia C. Godwin - Feb. 10, 1907, age 56 yrs.

LOT 10
Ave. 8
Owners - Sarah S. Hobday, W/H - Belle Bain, E/H

Sarah L. or S. Hobday - Dec. 3, 1904, age 53 yrs.
Walter E. or C. Hobday - June 4, 1889, age 51 yrs.
Belle P. Bain - Dec. 8, 1932, age 72 yrs.
Evelyn Bain - Oct. 23, 1945, age 83 yrs.
Edward C. Bain - Apr. 16, 1944, age 85 yrs.
Emma Bain - died May 31, 1942, age 53 yrs.

LOT 11
Ave. 8
Owner - M. A. Moore
Lucie K. Moore - Dec. 22, 1885, age 4 yrs.
Harriett S. Moore - Oct. 26, 1922, age 71 yrs.
Mallary A. Moore - Feb. 12, 1912, age 63 yrs.
Laura V. Godwin - Nov. 25, 1922, age 74 yrs.
Julia White Moore - Mar. 26, 1953, age 73 yrs.
Mallory Augustine Moore - Feb. 20, 1964.
Mary C. James - Jan. 15, 1898, age 69 yrs.
Joseph N. James - Feb. 7, 1898, age 37 yrs.
Summer A. Sherwood - Sept. 7, 1897, age 5 yrs. 3 mos.
2 graves - no names.
Mary A. Moore - Sept. 15, 19--, age 68 yrs.
Christian H. Moore - Nov. 30, 189-, age 6 mos.
Moore - stillborn of E. V. Moore, Dec. 5, 19--.
S. A. Sherwood - Sept. 27, 1897, age 3 yrs. 3 mos.
Mary Louise Moore - Nov. 19, 1899, age 27 yrs. 9 mos.

LOT 12
Ave. 8
Owner - Georgiana Sherwood
Virginia Day - Jan. 5, 1885, age 55 yrs.
Laura Day - Apr. 2, 1918, age 80 yrs.
Georgiana Day Sherwood - June 16, 1889, age 56 yrs.
Capt. William Sherwood - Jan. 23, 1908, age 82 yrs. (CSA).
Indie W. Sherwood - Oct. 8, 1915, age 71 yrs.
Smith A. Sherwood - Jan. 19, 1917, age 77 yrs.
Indie Sherwood Gayle - Feb. 8, 1940, age 65 yrs.
William E. Gayle - Apr. 7, 1929, age 63 yrs.

LOT 13
Ave. 8
Owner - H. B. Wilkins
Samuel S. Wilkins - Sept. 13, 1884, 10 mos.
Sarah L. Read Wilkins - Mar. 6, 1928, age 67 yrs.
Henry Boykins Wilkins - Jan. 27, 1939, age 84 yrs.
Eva W. Petters - moved Newport News June 12, 1953.

4

LOT 14
Ave. 8
Owner - W. G. Webb, E/H
5 graves - no names.
Annie L. Webb - July 25, 1892, age 8 yrs.
Whit H. Wilkins - June 4, 1886, age 3 mos.
Webb - stillborn, Apr. 10, 1924.
W. H. Massenberg - buried Aug. 30, 1889, age 33 yrs.
Harriett A. Massenberg - buried Feb. 26, 1893, age 68 yrs.

LOT 15
Ave. 8
Owners - A. J. Hopkins and A. B. Warren, W/H, Monument
Virginia Hopkins - July 12, 1910, age 72 yrs.
Andrew Hopkins - Feb. 17, 1912, age 79 yrs.
Lola Guedih - Oct. 3, 1951, age 67 yrs., E/H.
Mary P. Warren - Feb. 19, 1926, age 46 yrs.
Andrew B. Warren - Feb. 22, 1931, age 63 yrs.
Miller Infant - Aug. 18, 1934, age 13 hrs.
Lula M. Rodgers - Mar. 7, 1924, age 65 yrs.
Shelton - stillborn, Aug. 31, 1901, 1 day old.
T. R. Stratton - Feb. 26, 1906, age 46 yrs.

LOT 16
Ave. 8
Owners - Stephen Elliott and Mrs. Albert Landenberger, 327 E. Elmhurst, Peoria, Il.
Nettie Elliott - Jan. 20, 1884, age 18 yrs.
Nettie R. Elliott - June 19, 1884, age 5 mos.
Stephen Elliott - May 31, 1897, age 56 yrs.
Penelope Elliott - Jan. 11, 1901, age 69 yrs.
Thomas G. Elliott - Mar. 18, 1900, age 67 yrs.
Elliott Pool Fearing - Oct. 16, 1889, age 16 days.
Leonora Virginia Fearing - June 2, 1924, age 64 yrs.
Mary Elliott Shane - Jan. 14, 1929, age 71 yrs.
Vivian S. Brinkley - Jan. 17, 1949, age 64 yrs.
Harry F. Brinkley - Aug. 27, 1965.
T. Elliott buried - June 31, 189-, age 36 yrs.

LOT 17
Ave. 8
Owner - C. H. Stoakes
Mary Sue Stoakes Burgess - Apr. 16, 1912, age 41 yrs.
Pauline H. Stoakes - Feb. 15, 1917, age 79 yrs.
M. Annie Stoakes - Apr. 24, 1885.

C. H. Stoakes - July 8, 1883, age 40 yrs.
Julina J. Bilisoly - Feb. 7, 1958, age 81 yrs.
Annie B. Stoakes Billisoly - July 2, 1965.
James M. Pruden - Oct. 21, 1968 (vault).

LOT 18
Ave. 8
Owner - August Buff
Marie Bockringer - age 66 yrs.
Katherine Buff - Oct. 6, 1890, age 51 yrs.
August Buff - Aug. 11, 1897, age 60 yrs., CSA.
Henry F. A. Buff - 1869-1913, age 40 yrs.
Margaret Estell Buff - Dec. 13, 1974.
Charles D. Lane, Jr. - Mar. 2, 1984 (vault).
Harry L. Culpepper - Nov. 5, 1919.
Emma Paull Buff - Feb. 11, 1901, age 63 yrs.
H. L. Paull - June 5, 1895, age 61 yrs.
Louisa Armstrong - Aug. 12, 1890, age 42 yrs.

LOT 19
Ave. 8
Owner - H. J. Phillips
H. J. Phillips - Sept. 23, 1884, age 69 yrs.
Virginia H. Phillips - Mar. 7, 1900, age 79 yrs.
Annie M. Phillips - July 25, 1904, age 53 yrs.
Rosa M. Phillips - Aug. 3, 1942, age 91 yrs.
John J. Phillips - Apr. 2, 1902, age 57 yrs.

LOT 20
Old 107
Owner - K. R. Griffin
Kenneth Joseph Griffin - Oct. 13, 1915, age 45 yrs.
Lt. K. R. Griffin - Artillery CSA.
Kenneth Raynor Griffin - Mar. 29, 1912, age 70 yrs.
Alice A. Bourke Griffin - June 8, 1925, age 83 yrs.
Rosalie Holmes Griffin - Aug. 4, 1900, age 20 yrs.
Virginia Griffin Riddick - July 27, 1965.
Samuel B. Riddick - Dec. 20, 1980 (vault).

LOT 20
Ave. 1, Old 106
Owner - John B. Bourke
Adele B. Bagley - Apr. 21, 1970 (vault).
Walter L. Bilisoly - Apr. 26, 1918.
Laura V. Bourke - Nov. 15, 1927, age 88 yrs.

J. B. Bourke - July 1, 1910, age 73 yrs., CSA.
Joseph Bourke - Aug. 20, 1888, age 76 yrs.
Virginia A. Bourke - Aug. 22, 1887, age 67 yrs.
Rose Bourke Laurence - Aug. 8, 1873, age 34 yrs.
John M. Bourke - Aug. 8, 1861, age 44 yrs.
Mary Elise Bourke - June 22, 1893, age 77 yrs.

LOT 20
Ave. 1, Old 105
Owner - James L. Bilisoly
Robert, Elizabeth, Mary - infant children of F. Nash and C. Ruth
    Bilisoly.
Frank Nash Bilisoly - Jan. 12, 1947, age 78 yrs.
Ruth Hudgins Bilisoly - Mar. 23, 1957, age 89 yrs.
Joseph L. Bilisoly - Apr. 8, 1956, age 60 yrs.
Mary Trant Bilisoly - Aug. 18, 1973.
Joseph Lorenzo Bilisoly - 1904, age 63 yrs., 9th Va. Inf. CSA.
Elizabeth Bourke Bilisoly - 1934, age 90 yrs.

LOT 21
Ave. 1, Old 104
Owner - Samuel S. Peed
Samuel S. Peed - Nov. 15, 1895, age 59 yrs., 9th Va. CSA.
Elizabeth F. Peed - Nov. 25, 1913, age 74 yrs.
Doris Peed - Feb. 1, 1899, age 2 yrs. 7 mos.

LOT 22
Ave. 1, Old M
Owner - Edmund L. Barlow
Edmund L. Barlow - Oct. 12, 1929, age 61 yrs.
Sallie Werte Barlow - Dec. 30, 1950, age 87 yrs.
Nathaniel E. Adamson - Nov. 18, 1957, age 69 yrs.
Esther Adamson - May 5, 1952, age 58 yrs.
Reserved - Adamson
Evelyn Adamson - Dec. 5, 1984 (vault).
Vacant
Samuel Rogers Carey - Jan. 20, 1939, age 62 yrs.

LOT 23
Ave. 1
Owner - J. Davis Reed
J. Davis Reed - Sept. 1, 1952, age 86 yrs.
Anne Shaw Reed - Apr. 20, 1944, age 65 yrs.
Henry Shaw Reed - Apr. 8, 1955, age 44 yrs.

LOT 24 W
Ave. 1
Owner - R. A. Robertson
John Pickrell Robertson - son of Robert Angus Robertson and
    Dorothy Pickrell Robertson, Apr. 5, 1923-Aug. 3, 1943.
Dorothy McGlensey Pickrell - wife of Robert Angus Robertson,
    Mar. 30, 1893-Dec. 16, 1956.
Robert Angus Roberts - son of Mary C. Niemeyer and Robert
    Roberts, Feb. 23, 1895-July 6, 1954.
Mary Chandler Niemeyer - wife of Robert R. Robertson, Aug. 6,
    1865-Nov. 26, 1952.
Dorothy Pickett - Sept. 30, 1987 (vault).

LOT 25
Old J
*Owners - S. S. Nottingham - Transferred Jan. 22, 1969, to
    Wimbrough and Sons, sold four graves to Col. and Mrs. John
    C. Healey, Sept. 25, 1973.*
Frances Yardley Nottingham - Jan. 29, 1968, age 83 yrs. (vault).
Smith Severn Nottingham - Oct. 23, 1919, age 67 yrs.
Fanny Bain Nottingham - Nov. 13, 1923, age 71 yrs.
Sallie B. Nottingham - Nov. 13, 1952, age 61 yrs.
Willie Cherry Nottingham - Nov. 10, 1965.
3 graves - Hilton.
4 graves - Healey.

LOT 27
Ave. 1, Old H
Owner - Goodrich Hatton
Goodrich Hatton - Apr. 2, 1929, age 66 yrs.
Mary Watts Hatton - Apr. 22, 1947, age 75 yrs.

LOT 28
Ave. 1, Old G
Owner - Jane E. Mules
R. O. B. Mules - Nov. 30, 1911, age 48 yrs.
Jane E. Mules - Dec. 17, 1911, age 46 yrs.

LOT 29
Ave. 1, Old G
Owner - S. P. Wigg
Sam Patterson Wigg - Apr. 11, 1913, age 50 yrs.
Annie McLean Wigg - Nov. 8, 1926, age 66 yrs.
Sam P. Wigg - buried Feb. 27, 1979.

James L. Kirby - Jan. 6, 1963.
James L. Kirby - disinterred Mar. 22, 1978.

LOT 30
Old F
Owner - John W. H. Porter
Hunter Ball Porter - June 18, 1912, age 27 yrs., 1st Lt. USA.
John W. H. Porter - May 20, 1916, age 74 yrs., Reg. Va. CSA.
Elizabeth Ball Porter - July 11, 1931, age 85 yrs.
John Ridgely Porter - July 16, 1942, age 90 yrs.
Augusta M. Porter - Oct. 4, 1950, age 66 yrs.

LOT 31
Ave. 1, Old E
Owners - C. E. Adams and R. M. Burford
Charles Emmette Adams, Jr. - Nov. 4, 1934, age 41 yrs.
Permella O. Adams - Dec. 1, 1936, age 68 yrs.
Charles Emmette Adams - June 10, 1928, age 61 yrs.
David Madison Etheridge - Mar. 6, 1912, age 56 yrs.
David William Granville Whitehurst - 1832-1915, age 82 yrs.,
    41st Va. Inf. CSA.
Permelia Owens Whitehurst - Jan. 7, 1925, age 83 yrs.
Mary Burford - Oct. 10, 1942, age 80 yrs.
Robert Milton Burford - Jan. 16, 1918, age 70 yrs.
Norman O. W. Adams - Jan. 8, 1964.
Sarah Adams - Nov. 16, 1974 (vault).

LOT 32
Old D
Owner - Washington Reed
13 graves - no names.
Reed - infant, May 28, 1920, age 2 hrs old.
Washington Reed - died June 11, 1952, body moved from Nor-
    folk Apr. 21, 1954.
Florence B. Reed - Nov. 17, 1964.
George Frank Williams - Oct. 15, 1966.
Gordon A. Griffin - Aug. 23, 1985.
William Murdaugh Reed - Mar. 26, 1976.

LOT 33
Ave. 1, Old C
Owners - Clarence T., Virginius T., and Raymond Benson Peed
Lewis W. Blow - Sept. 3, 1959, age 88 yrs.
Bessie E. Blow - July 15, 1961, age 75 yrs.
Adelia Peed - Dec. 6, 1982.

Ralph D. Peed - Nov. 17, 1955, age 65 yrs.
Virginius T. Peed - 1847-1910, age 62 yrs.
Hugh D. Peed - July 29, 1945, age 64 yrs.
Raymond Peed - Dec. 20, 1949, age 74 yrs.
Florence A. Peed - Mar. 5, 1910, age 60 yrs.
Florence Adrienne Dewitt - infant, Jan. 29, 1934.
Infant - June 6, 1943.

LOT 34
Ave. 1, Old B
Owner - J. W. Old
Jonathan W. Old - Mar. 15, 1934, age 80 yrs.
Richard Old - disinterred from Oak Grove and reinterred Cedar
    Grove, Dec. 7, 1934.
Richard Paxton Old - Dec. 7, 1934.
Jonathan W. Old - (name interred twice) Mar. 15, 1934, age 80
    yrs.
Claudia Paxton Old - Dec. 6, 1946, age 86 yrs.
Note: Richard Paxton Old - son of Mr. Jonathan W. Old and
    Mrs. Claudia Paxton Old - who died Sat. night at 9:15, took
    place this morning at 11 A.M. in Trinity Church. Rev. A. C.
    Thompson, pastor of the church officiating, interment Oak
    Grove.
    Large attendance of friends and relatives of the boy who
    was very popular with his companions. He was only 17 yrs.
    and 14 mos. when he died. Relatives were present from
    Edenton, North Carolina, the home of Richard's mother
    where he was very widely known, many floral decorations.
    Pallbearers: Collins Hill, Stuart Silvester, Henry Etheridge
    and R. S. Gayle.

LOT 35
Ave. 1, Old B
Owner - W. M. Pugh
Warner Marion Pugh - Oct. 17, 1933, age 66 yrs.
Mary Butt Pugh - Feb. 4, 1944, age 69 yrs.
Waverly R. Winborne - Aug. 29, 1961, age 19 yrs.
Grace Lane Pugh - Oct. 10, 1967 (vault).
Sumner Riddick Pugh - Feb. 11, 1966.
Helen P. Pugh - Sept. 16, 1982 (vault).

LOT 36
Ave. 1, Old A
Owners - W. E. Flournoy, sold Louise Brown, Certificate 277.
W. Edward Flournoy - May 4, 1948, age 71 yrs.

Mary Bruce Flournoy - Nov. 2, 1945, age 68 yrs.
Mary F. Brown - Mar. 4, 1949, age 38 yrs.
Bruce Flournoy - Jan. 29, 1913, age 4 yrs.
G. W. Foote - buried 1906, infant.
McDowell Foote Harris - July 6, 1976.
Waverly R. Winborne - Apr. 6, 1970.
Mary Wilson Pugh Winborne - Feb. 9, 1970.

LOT 37
Ave. 1, Old 31
Owner - John H. Hall
Annes Hart - Jan. 11, 1893, 6 days old.
Mary A. Lewis - Oct. 3, 1885, infant.
Margaret Gayle - Sept. 24, 1889, age 92 yrs.
John T. Nelms - Feb. 28, 1888, age 57 yrs.
Emily C. Nelms - Nov. 10, 1899, age 65 yrs.
Mary C. Hall - Jan. 23, 1941, age 85 yrs.
John Hopkins Hall - 1853-1922, age 69 yrs.
4 graves - no names.

LOT 38
Ave. 2, Old 30
Owner - Julia H. Hargrove
Martha Tatem Brinkley - Dec. 10, 1905.
Wade Hampton Brinkley - July 21, 1907.
Alice H. Payne - 1873-1930, age 56 yrs.
Willis W. Hargrove, Jr. - 1910-1932, age 21 yrs.
Willis Hargrove - July 29, 1939, age 58 yrs.
Violet S. Hargrove - Feb. 26, 1958, age 71 yrs.
Mary H. Brinkley - Nov. 8, 1961, age 82 yrs.
Wade H. Brinkley - 1876-1936, age 59 yrs.
Willis W. Hargrove - Feb. 14, 1906, age 64 yrs.
Julia Tatem Hargrove - July 14, 1909, age 66 yrs.
Robert T. Hargrove - 1870-1910, age 39 yrs.
Robert T. Hargrove, Jr. - 1904-1924, age 19 yrs.
Emily Carney Hargrove - Feb. 9, 1967 (vault).

LOT 39
Old 31
Owner - T. B. Bartee
T. B. Bartee - June 19, 1897, age 71 yrs., CSA.

LOT 40
Ave. 2, Old 29
Owner - William H. Brittingham

Miss Mary B. Brittingham - Sept. 1, 1940, age 63 yrs. 8 mos.
Sallie Brickhouse Brittingham - Sept. 18, 1935, age 91 yrs.
William H. Brittingham - Feb. 10, 1907, age 70 yrs., 9th Va. Inf. CSA.
Thomas V. Brittingham - Mar. 12, 1901, age 55 yrs.
Annis Brittingham - Mar. 30, 1890, age 56 yrs.
Mary Edith Brittingham - Sept. 9, 1928, age 4 yrs. 10 mos.
Stillborn of P. B. Brittingham - Jan. 15, 1910.
Stillborn of William V. Brittingham - Nov. 11, 1914.

LOT 41
Ave. 1
Owner - John T. Laurence
Cora Frances Betzill - 1869-1902, age 29 yrs.
Mary Elizabeth Laurence - 1852-1887, age 35 yrs.
Mary Frances Laurence - Dec. 15, 1945, age 67 yrs.
C. C. Laurence - Oct. 3, 1895, age 27 yrs.
1 grave - no name.
Sarah F. Laurence - June 26, 1895, age 38 yrs.
John T. Laurence - Feb. 10, 1936, age 85 yrs.
William T. Dewberry - Aug. 3, 1923, age 55 yrs.
C. Wayne Petzinger - Nov. 17, 1898.
William J. Petzinger - May 24, 1898.
Hannah Betzel - Mar. 23, 1902, age 7 mos.

LOT 42
Ave. 2, Old 29
Owner - Mary V. Johnston
W. M. Smith - May 8, 1949, age 78 yrs.
Frances Smith - Aug. 9, 1961, age 86 yrs.
Anna Dorothy Smith - age 7 mos.
Margaret J. Smith - June 15, 1908, age 9 yrs.
M. B. Johnston - buried May 29, 1896, age 7 mos.
John A. Smith - buried June 20, 1892, age 15 days.
Mayor Francis C. Johnston - 1845-1925, CSA.
Mary Virginia Johnston - 1848-1915, age 66 yrs.
Anna Johnston - died Apr. 18, 1941, age 73 yrs.

LOT 43
Ave. 1, Old 33
Owner - Celestia P. Hartt
Bury Evelyn Hartt Mona Sect.
Katherine A. Hartt - Oct. 3, 1974 (vault).
Katherine Hartt - died Jan. 1, 1947, age 79 yrs.
William H. Hartt - died Jan. 17, 1930, age 72 yrs.

Grace C. Hartt - died Aug. 14, 1868, age 9 yrs.
Celestia P. Hartt - died June 30, 1906.
Evelyn Hartt - Mar. 21, 1897, age 43 yrs.

LOT 44
Ave. 2, Old 28
Owner - R. D. Hamilton
Mary E. Martin - 1843-1903, age 60 yrs.
E. Frank DeBerry - Mar. 17, 1965.
Mary Ethel Hamilton - 1879-1880, age 1 yr.
Richard Dabney Hamilton - 1855-1930, age 75 yrs.
Ella Hamilton - Nov. 15, 1941, age 82 yrs.
Rev. George M. Wright - July 23, 1885, age 45 yrs.
Bedell Hamilton - 1810-1895, age 85 yrs.
Mary Ann Hamilton - 1821-1887, age 65 yrs.
Isabelle Alvira Smith - 1831-1903, age 66 yrs.
Lillian H. Wood - cremated Feb. 9, 1965.

LOT 45
Ave. 1, Old 33
Owner - James H. Toomer
Lamar Chappell Toomer - Oct. 9, 1939, age 65 yrs.
James Hodges Toomer - June 7, 1929, age 50 yrs.
Loretta M. Toomer - Oct. 21, 1956, age 79 yrs.
Katherine Toomer - June 28, 1984, age 96 yrs.
Rebecca Dorothy Chappell Toomer - Sept. 18, 1915, age 71 yrs.
James Hodges Toomer - Jan. 22, 1915, age 80 yrs., CSA.
James H. Toomer - Mar. 14, 1943, age 22 yrs.
Sarah B. Elam - July 5, 1888 age 6 mos.

LOT 46
Ave. 2, Old 27
*Owners - William Appenzeller, N/H (North Half) - P. C. Asser-
son, S/H (South Half)*
William H. Appenzeller - buried Sept. 7, 1892, age 7 mos.
Edith Rose Asserson - Feb. 3, 1880, age 6 yrs. 3 mos.
Willie F. Appenzeller - 1874-1881.
Mattie Lester - Dec. 19, 1911, age 65 yrs.
Nettie Appenzeller Gildersleve - Jan. 17, 1885, age 20 yrs.
Asser Asserson - Dec. 8, 1878, age 52 yrs.
William H. Appenzeller - Dec. 21, 1890, age 61 yrs.

LOT 47
Ave. 1, Old 34
Owner - James Parrish

James S. Parrish - July 22, 1940, age 69 yrs. 11 mos.
Dr. Hugh Parrish - Oct. 7, 1935, age 63 yrs.
Wortley Parrish - Mar. 7, 1884, age 5 yrs.
Dr. James Parrish - Jan. 25, 1894, age 54 yrs., Surgeon CSA.
Alice T. Parrish - Dec. 25, 1912, age 71 yrs.
Frederick M. Parrish - Nov. 21, 1909, age 26 yrs.
Francis W. Parrish - buried Mar. 8, 1884, age 4 yrs.
Eliza Jane Parrish - Jan. 7, 1888, age 61 yrs. 9 mos.
Alice Toomer Parrish - July 6, 1921, age 5 1/2 yrs.
Winston Parrish - Aug. 20, 1920, age 44.
Elizabeth Pendleton Parrish - Jan. 7, 1888, age 64.

LOT 48
Ave. 2, Old 26
Owner - J. M. Barrett
Josephine Taylor - Apr. 1, 1930, age 76 yrs.
Sarah Catherine Barrett - Jan. 29, 1911, age 25 yrs.
R. R. Taylor - Feb. 12, 1897, age 67 yrs.
George Taylor child - buried Aug. 20, 1893, age 2 days.
C. R. Taylor - buried Dec. 12, 1895, age 10 mos.
Charles Taylor - Feb. 7, 1943, age 63 yrs.
Sarah A. Barrett - June 17, 1882, age 60 yrs.
James Madison Barrett - July 8, 1891, age 77 yrs.
Indiana Barrett - Oct. 13, 1947, age 86 yrs.

LOT 49
Ave. 1, Old 35
Owner - John H. Hume
Charles G. Hume - Sept. 7, 1949, age 72 yrs.
Joseph G. Hume - July 29, 1935, age 46 yrs.
Anna P. Hume - 1850-1919.
John H. Hume - 1844-1899, Signal Corp CSA.
Jennie Braxton Hume - 1869-1880, age 10 yrs.

LOT 50
Ave. 2, Old 26
Owner - J. N. Gray, S/H
Alexander Gray - 1831-1909, age 77 yrs.
J. N. Gray - May 24, 1882, age 49 yrs.
Theopolus Nicholson - buried Feb. 3, 1891, age 45 yrs.

LOT 51
Ave. 1, Old 36
Owner - Mrs. Kemp Plummer
Kemp Plummer - Nov. 3, 1871-Aug. 8, 1936.

Ruth W. Plummer - May 27, 1985 (vault).
Josephine W. Plummer - Nov. 25, 1974.
Leaven Bristor Plummer - Mar. 29, 1966.
Infant of L. J. and N. R. Plummer.
Elsie Plummer Crocker - May 18, 1934, age 60 yrs.
Maj. K. Plummer - died Sept. 18, 1888, age 56 yrs.
Ann G. Plummer - 1844-1912.
Sallie E. Plummer - 1868-1929.
Esther P. Crocker - 1873-1934.
Frank Lee Crocker - Oct. 23, 1927, age 62 yrs.
Annie T. Plummer - Feb. 17, 1912, age 68 yrs.
Infant of L. J. and N. J. Plummer - Nov. 5, 1914, buried Nov. 6, 1914.
Salla F. Plummer - May 31, 1929, age 61 yrs.
Kemp Plummer - Aug. 8, 1936, age 64 yrs.

LOT 52
Ave. 2, Old 25
Owners - Williamson Smith, N/H - C. L. Reiger, S/H
Elizabeth Smith - June 18, 1948, age 85 yrs.
Williamson Smith - Nov. 13, 1909, age 66 yrs. 9 mos.
Mary Isabelle Smith - June 5, 1914, age 44 yrs.
Rosalie T. Smith - Jan. 30, 1888, age 39 yrs.
Charles A. Reiger - Oct. 14, 1912, age 61 yrs.
Caroline Reiger - May 21, 1907, age 92 yrs.
Frank C. Reiger - Feb. 8, 1928, age 83 yrs.

LOT 53
Ave. 1, Old S1 and T1
Owner - Richard Cox
Matilda S. Cox - Mar. 13, 1894, age 76 yrs.
Richard Cox - Dec. 2, 1893, age 77 yrs.
Charles S. Cox - Jan. 15, 1874, age 28 yrs.
Richard W. Cox - Oct. 31, 1899, age 52 yrs.
Richard Cox Barlow - Jan. 27, 1904, age 28 yrs.
Thomas S. Barlow - June 4, 1887, age 11 mos.
Maggie Barlow - Oct. 14, 1873, age 7 yrs.
Matilda C. Barlow - July 13, 1905, age 36 yrs.

LOT 53
Ave. 2, Old T1 and S1
Owner - Richard Cox
John W. Cox - Sept. 7, 1900, age 46 yrs.
John Francis Benson - 1873-1935, age 61 yrs.
Cassel Barlow Benson - Jan. 10, 1961, age 80 yrs.

Annie C. Barlow - Oct. 4, 1954, age 81 yrs.
Thomas Joel Barlow - Nov. 8, 1923, age 81 yrs.
Annie M. Barlow - Aug. 29, 1916, age 73 yrs.
C. H. Barlow, M.D. - July 21, 1924, age 46 yrs.

LOT 54
Ave. 1, Old C
Owners - Stroud - Proctor - Mears
William Stroud - Jan. 23, 1910, age 93 yrs.
Adelia Ann Stroud - Nov. 10, 1918, age 87 yrs.
Virgie Proctor - Dec. 15, 1960, age 82 yrs.
Robert Proctor - July 10 1897, age 81 yrs.
Luzerne E. Proctor - Feb. 7, 1907, age 86 yrs.
James C. Proctor, Jr. - died May 9, 1960, age 79 yrs.
James C. Proctor - Apr. 11, 1919, age 75 yrs.
Maria E. White Proctor - Dec. 31, 1928, age 83 yrs.
Mary Proctor - July 24, 1915.
Ruth D. Proctor - Jan. 1, 1958, age 79 yrs.
Proctor - stillborn, May 14, 1886.

LOT 55
Ave. 2, Old E
Owner - John Hobday
John R. Hobday - Sept. 28, 1860, age 25 yrs.
Lena Hobday Fraser - 1857-1915, age 57 yrs.
R. B. Fraser - 1855-1913, age 57 yrs.
Wesley Hobday - Nov. 6, 1884, age 54 yrs.
Virginia A. Higginbotham - Jan. 6, 1910, age 76 yrs.
John Hobday Lawrence - Nov. 15, 1966, age 77 yrs.
Edwynna Harris Lawrence - July 17, 1967 (vault).
Adelade Virginia Jobson - Apr. 17, 1905, age 47 yrs.
Laura Virginia Hobday - May 12, 1908, age 71 yrs.
Bessie Virginia Jobson - age 9 mos.
Leslie J. Royal - Sept. 7, 1905, age 7 mos.

LOT 56
Ave. 1, Old B
Owner - D. W. Ballentine
Carrie V. P. Ballentine - Mar. 10, 1961, age 72 yrs.
James R. Ballentine - Apr. 5, 1960, age 72 yrs.
Reserved - Brownley
A. W. Ballentine - Dec. 14, 1889, age 7 mos. 12 days.
Hudgins - stillborn, Apr. 7, 1926.
David T. Ballentine - Jan. 1, 1955, age 71 yrs.
Jay B. Creech - Dec. 6, 1957, age 37 yrs.

Reserved - Brownley
Ruth M. Ballentine - Sept. 7, 1924, age 64 yrs.
D. W. Ballentine - Oct. 23, 1916, age 73 yrs., 9th Va. Inf. CSA.
Ardelsy Meyers Ballentine - Sept. 23, 1881, monument.

LOT 57
Old D
Owner - Mrs. R. D. Peed
R. W. Peed - CSA.
J. Peed - CSA.

LOT 58
Ave. 1, Old A6
Owner - James G. Bain
Emily Butler Bain - buried Oct. 5, 1896, age 58 yrs.
James Gaskins Bain - Feb. 25, 1889, age 53 yrs.
McKay Bain - Dec. 8, 1942, age 82 yrs.
Mrs. Nancy Forbes Owens - Nov. 7, 1939, age 78 yrs. 10 mos.
Thomas C. Owens - Feb. 21, 1933, age 70 yrs.
Sally G. Forbes - Aug. 26, 1925, age 70 yrs.
Sarah Ann Bain Forbes - Sept. 23, 1893, age 69 yrs.
Nester Howard Forbes - 1817-1885, age 68 yrs., CSA.

LOT 58
Ave. 2, Old A12
Owner - Capt. Thomas A. Bain
Thomas A. B. Hall - July 24, 1915.
Lillie T. Bain - June 2, 1891, age 31 yrs.
Capt. Thomas A. Bain - Oct. 18, 1877, age 47 yrs.
Indiana M. Bain - Aug. 26, 1893, age 64 yrs.
James Laurence Smith - Aug. 29, 1962.
Dorothy L. Smith - Feb. 28, 1973 (vault).
Ambrose H. Lindsay, Jr. - Dec. 8, 1906, age 37 yrs.
Indiana Bain Lindsay - Dec. 25, 1926, age 55 yrs.
John Howard Hall - Apr. 13, 1925, age 68 yrs.
Mary A. Bain Hall - Oct. 6, 1923, age 65 yrs.
Harry R. Bain - July 1869.
Ruth Bain - Feb. 1867.
Alice M. Bain - Aug. 1863.
Thomas A. Bain, Jr. - July 1856.
Monument

LOT 58
Ave. 2, Old 222
Owner - George M. Bain

Nannie Cowell Bain - Nov. 17, 1864, age 6 yrs.
Willie Bain - June 24, 1864, age 14 yrs.
William Cherry Bain - Nov. 20, 1867, age 1 yr.
Margaret McKenza Nottingham - June 21, 1883, age 1 yr.
Sally Bain Pryor - 1860-1887, age 27 yrs.
Sally Bain Pryor - 1887-1888, age 6 mos.
George M. Bain, Jr. - buried July 3, 1892, age 9 yrs. 8 mos.
George M. Bain - Oct. 4, 1906, age 80 yrs.
Willie F. C. Bain - Nov. 26, 1909, age 82 yrs.
George McK. Bain - June 13, 1916, age 57 yrs.
Mary Gaskins Barnard - Aug. 19, 1913, age 67 yrs.
Mary Hurt Bain - Nov. 9, 1917, age 61 yrs.

LOT 58
Ave. 1, Old A5
Owner - R. T. K. Bain
Matilda Winston Daughtry Bain - Feb. 9, 1930, age 54 yrs.
Kenneth A. Bain "Judge" - Nov. 25, 1944, age 85 yrs.
Matilda Winston Bain - Aug. 24, 1902, age 8 mos.
Thomas Clayton
Virginia Bain - Mar. 12, 1942, age 43 yrs.
Forrest Bain - Jan. 15, 1874, age 7 yrs.
Amelia Benson Bain - Nov. 6, 1870, age 31 yrs.
Robert T. K. Bain - Sept. 11, 1901, age 62 yrs.

LOT 59
Ave. 1, Old A4
Owner - M. D. Eastwood
Mary Louise Vaughan - 1910-1914, age 3 yrs.
J. Powell Eastwood - 1873-1909, age 35 yrs.
Carrie Eastwood - Oct. 4, 1946, age 79 yrs.
William T. Eastwood - 1870-1933, age 63 yrs.
Mary Ann Eastwood - 1839-1901, age 63 yrs.
Matthew D. Eastwood - 1831-1905, age 74 yrs.
M. Lee Eastwood - 1861-1921, age 59 yrs.
Annie Elizabeth Eastwood - Nov. 1, 1970 (vault).

LOT 60
Ave. 2, Old A11
Owner - John Nash
Eleanor C. Ball - Sept. 19, 1986 (vault).
Mary Susan Nash Woodley - July 20, 1866, age 33 yrs.
1 grave - no name.
V. W. Nash - age 52 yrs., 9th Va. Inf. CSA.
Ridley A. Turner - Apr. 19, 1884, age 88 yrs., born 1795 or 1796.

Sophia Lucretia Weston - 1919, age 5 days.
Nannie Lucretia Woodley Chapman - Jan. 5, 1933, age 77 yrs.
Mary Susan Woodley - Sept. 18, 1878, age 19 yrs.
Lizzie Edwards Woodley - Apr. 3, 1919, age 58 yrs.
Dr. Joseph Rhea Woodley - Sept. 29, 1897, age 68 yrs., Lt.
    Signal Corp. CSA.
Annie W. Woodley - Dec. 4, 1918, age 79 yrs.

LOT 61
Ave. 1, Old A3
Owner - A. L. Bilisoly
Eliza A. Bilisoly - July 8, 1895, age 90 yrs.
Joseph A. Bilisoly - Dec. 15, 1880, age 80 yrs.
Dr. Antonio L. Bilisoly - Nov. 20, 1907, age 71 yrs., 9th Va. Inf.
    CSA.
Annie Camm Bilisoly - July 30, 1905, age 73 yrs.
Mrs. Catherine Camm - Aug. 30, 1855, age 50 yrs.
Robert C. Hill - June 4, 1911, age 4 mos.
Raymond S. - 1869-1875.
Annie Camm - 1872-1874.
Willie C. - 1867-1868.
Robert Lelse - Aug. 14, 1866.
Antonio J. - Jan. 17, 1861.
Eleanor Stuart Niemeyer - Feb. 17, 1927, age 6 yrs.
Lucrece Bilisoly Niemeyer - Dec. 22, 1819, age 55 yrs.
J. Fred Niemeyer - Apr. 24, 1930, age 65 yrs.

LOT 62
Ave. 2, Old A10
Owner - John Nash
Richard Gregory Hume - June 29, 1918, age 41 yrs.
John Nash Hume - Aug. 19, 1937, age 68 yrs.
Richard Gregory Hume - Dec. 8, 1878, CSA.
Sarah Lucretia Hume - Aug. 11, 1905.
Thomas Hume - Feb. 21, 1915, age 44 yrs.
Mary Gregory Hume - Jan. 24, 1876, age 4 yrs.
Nancy Collins - Sept. 28, 1885, age 1 yr., child of F. A. Nash.
Farlie Patton - Mar. 29, 1897, age 5 yrs., child of F. A. Nash.
Fairlie Patton Nash - Apr. 6, 1914, age 62 yrs.
Fannie A. Nash - Oct. 11, 1932, age 78 yrs.
Annie C. Nash - July 13, 1916, age 62 yrs.
John Nash - June 24, 1884, age 78 yrs.
Ann L. Nash - Sept. 12, 1898, age 89 yrs.

LOT 63
Ave. 1, Old A2
Owner - Alexander Skeeter
Infant R. L. Skeeter - stillborn, Aug. 21, 1891.
Maggie Skeeter - July 26, 1892, age 21 days.
Robert Skeeter - May 17, 1894, 2 mos.
Mary E. Skeeter - Jan. 10, 1893, 2 mos.
Robert E. L. Skeeter - Aug. 26, 1900, age 35 yrs. 10 mos.
Clyd Shaver - buried Apr. 22, 1891, age 2 mos.
Monument
Lavinia S. Morris - Dec. 24, 1947, age 88 yrs.
John W. Morris - Mar. 16, 1952, age 92 yrs.
Mattie S. Duke - Jan. 4, 1909, age 47 yrs.
Sarah M. Skeeter - Aug. 2, 1925, age 89 yrs.
Alexander Skeeter - Jan. 28, 1896, age 58 yrs., CSA.
Sallie H. R. Skeeter - Mar. 28, 1900, age 34 yrs.
V. Skeeter - Jan. 27, 1896, age 58 yrs.
Eugene J. Skeeter - May 15, 1901, age 26 yrs.
Infant of J. W. and L. M. Morris - Apr. 22, 1891, age 2 mos.

LOT 64
Ave. 2, Old A9
Owner - William Schroeder
Margaret H. Schroder - Sept. 20, 1923, age 47 yrs.
Dr. William Charles Schroder - Feb. 18, 1937, age 60 yrs.
Lucrece Sophia Schroeder - Apr. 9, 1973 (vault).
Mary F. Schroeder - Apr. 30, 1950, age 82 yrs.
Mary Elizabeth Schroeder - 1842-1907, age 65 yrs.
Charles Schroeder - 1836-1910, age 74 yrs., Chief Engr. CSN.
William Schroeder - 1831-1908, age 77 yrs.
Lucrece Schroeder - 1824-1904, age 80 yrs.

LOT 65
Ave. 1, Old A1
Owner - F. R. Benson
Monument
Alice C. Benson - Sept. 9, 1921, age 53 yrs.
Francis R. Benson - Nov. 15, 1900, age 65 yrs., CSA.
Lizzie A. Benson - Aug. 16, 1927, age 74 yrs.
Moss W. Armistead - Aug. 2, 1878, age 66 yrs.
Alice C. Armistead Benson - Nov. 12, 1869, age 27 yrs.
Dora Benson - Oct. 23, 1869.

LOT 66
Ave. 2, Old A8

Owner - C. W. Murdaugh
James Murdaugh - 1857-1886, age 29 yrs.
Mary Murdaugh Cross - 1838-1899, age 60 yrs.
George Hipkins Murdaugh - 1869-1925, age 55 yrs.
Josiah Murdaugh - age 73, died Maryview Hospital Jan. 6, 1955.
James Murdaugh - 1799-1870, age 70 yrs.
Mary P. Murdaugh - 1805-1878, age 72 yrs.
Claudius W. Murdaugh - 1828-1898, age 70 yrs., Capt. 61st Inf.
   CSA.
Eugenia D. Murdaugh - 1834-1920, age 85 yrs.
William Calvert Murdaugh - 1876-1895, age 18 yrs.

LOT 67
Ave. A, Old 9
Owners - Atkinson and George W. Reynolds
Louis W. Atkinson - 1724 A. St., Washington, D.C., East Section.
George W. Reynolds - Feb. 1, 1897, age 85 yrs.
Clyde C. Savage - buried Apr. 5, 1897, age 9 yrs.
Capt. A. Portlock - CSA.
1 grave - no name.
1 grave - no name.
S. Tabb Reynolds - May 23, 1899, age 76 yrs.
Note: South Half in West End of Lot 67 purchased by Frank N.
   Bilisoly from Laura P. Atkinson Oct. 17, 1956, sold to Irving
   A. Johnson, Jr., June 24, 1971.

LOT 68
Ave. 2, Old A7
Owner - Judge J. F. Crocker
Margaret E. Hodges - Nov. 18, 1948, age 86 yrs.
Judge James F. Crocker - 1828-1917, age 89 yrs., Adj. 9th Va.
   Inf. CSA
Margaret Jane Crocker - July 25, 1896, age 58 yrs.
James Hodges Crocker - Aug. 12, 1868, age 7 yrs.
Emma Adelaide Hodges - Mar. 24, 1910, age 76 yrs.
Susie G. Hodges Baker - died Jan. 22, 1891.
Little Mary Baker - Aug. 19, 1890.
Dr. Archibald Atkinson - 1832-1903, age 71 yrs., Surgeon Wise
   Brigade CSA.
Mary Elizabeth Atkinson - 1839-1914, age 74 yrs.
Francis Hill Powell - 1805-1874.

LOT 69
Ave. 1, Old 13
Owners - Armistead and Holt

21

Rebecca C. Armistead - buried Dec. 21, 1892, age 8 yrs.
Armistead - stillborn, buried Sept. 15, 1890.
Rebecca A. Armistead - 1816-1893, age 76 yrs.
M. W. Armistead - 1811-1878, age 66 yrs.
William Holt - Apr. 26, 1856, age 46 yrs.
Willie, William, Mary, Elizabeth, Ida, Willie, Rebecca - infants of Rebecca A. and Moss W. Armistead.
William, Elizah, Aldan, Kate - infants of William and Lavenia Armistead.
Monument

LOT 70
Ave. 2, Old 27
Owner - George R. Trant
Virginia Young Trant - buried Sept. 21, 1893, age 28 yrs.
Tapley W. Young - died Jan. 16, 1904, age 71 yrs.
Sarah B. Trant - buried Jan. 20, 1893, age 40 yrs.
Annie Potter Young - buried Nov. 6, 1884, age 70 yrs.
Virginia Boykins Trant - died Oct. 3, 1893, age 28 yrs.
Capt. R. V. Boykin - Coms. Dept CSA.
George R. Trant - 1844-1904, age 59 yrs., 5th Cal. CSA.
Emma Boykin Culver or Culner - Feb. 2, 1907, age 62 yrs.

LOT 71
Ave. 1, Old 2
Owner - M. S. Latimer
Susannah Latimer - April 20, 1855, age 54 yrs.
Jane L. Latimer - Aug. 18, 1847, age 42 yrs.
J. W. Latimer - June 12, 1845, age 5 mos. 3 days.
James Pendergast Latimer - Feb. 6, 1842, age 2 yrs. 7 mos.

LOT 72
Ave. 2, Old 26
Owner - Lewis Thomas
Mary S. Thomas - Sept. 26, 1841.
Julia S. Chadwick - Feb. 15, 1878.
E. Waller Chadwick - 1876-1933, age 56 yrs.
Thomas Infant - Mar. 27, 1920, age 3 days.
Elizabeth W. Thomas - Jan. 26, 1888, age 84 yrs.
Lt. L. W. Thomas - Sept. 14, 1890, age 51 yrs., 26th Va. Inf. CSA.
Elizabeth F. Thomas - Jan. 19, 1879, age 60 or 66 yrs.
J. W. Thomas - Jan. 14, 1909, age 63 yrs., CSA.
John Lewis Thomas Jr. - June 22, 1912, age 2 mos.
Baby Thomas - died Sept. 24, 1946.

J. Lewis Thomas - Nov. 9, 1959, age 82 yrs.
Eleanor Abbitt Thomas - Apr. 26, 1972.

LOT 73
Ave. 1, Old 11
Owner - A. M. Tabb
Beulah T. Gayle - died June 20, 1960, age 68 yrs.
Nathaniel G. Gayle the 3rd - Nov. 17, 1963.
Johnson M. Tabb - Apr. 8, 1895, age 54 yrs.
Alexander Cunningham - 1776-1856.
Eliza Tabb - 1813-1881.
Henry A. Tabb - 1808-1882.
Lt. N. G. Gayle - 9th Va. Inf. CSA.
Katie G. Gayle - died Oct. 11, 1893, age 16 yrs. and 11 mos.
C. Tabb - CSA (Charles).
Sarah F. Gayle - Apr. 28, 1906, age 61 yrs.
Note: Henry A. Tabb was brother to Augustine Moore Tabb and
   son of Henry Tabb and Diana Moore Tabb and father of seven
   known children.

LOT 74
Ave. 2, Old 25
Owners - Simmons, N/H - Mary Gardner, S/H
Henry Gardner - July 17, 1859, age 50 yrs.
Mary Gardner - June 8, 1885, age 72 yrs.
Margaret Bullock - July 15, 1905.
George S. Bullock - Dec. 29, 1901, age 72 yrs.
Mollie E. Griggs - buried May 18, 1898, age 30 yrs.
4 graves - no names.
Rebecca L. Hingerty - Jan. 19, 1861, age 19 yrs.
Mollie F. McGellan Hingerty - Aug. 28, 1863.
Rosa Thomas and infant - May 15, 1842, age 32 yrs.

LOT 75
Ave. 1, Old 10
Owner - W. G. Staples, N/H
Gabella Grant - Feb. 9, 1901, age 69 yrs.
1 grave - no name.

LOT 76
Old 24
Owners - William Goodson, N/H - R. G. Staples, S/H
Eliza R. Staples - Feb. 9, 1923, age 70 yrs.
Annie K. Staples - Mar. 13, 1907, age 72 yrs.
Hattie M. Staples - June 27, 1887, age 25 yrs.

3 graves - no names.
Major R. G. Staples - June 20, 1891, age 58 yrs.
Foster Staples - Jan. 10, 1949, age 64 yrs.
Lelia Gatling Staples - Jan. 15, 1975.
B. W. Seymore - stillborn, May 23, 1889.
Kenny A. Seymore - Sept. 8, 1886, age 1 mo.
Robert C. Joiley - buried May 31, 1903, age 12 hrs.
A. H. Goodson - buried Dec. 1, 1894, age 66 yrs.
Joseph A. Goodson - buried Oct. 27, 1883, age 51 yrs.
Thomas B. Cuthrell - Aug. 19, 1909, age 7 days.

LOT 77
Ave. 1, Old 10
Owner - I. T. Van Patton
Smith Steicer Van Patton - infant.
Sarah F. Smith - 1840-1923, age 83 yrs.
Margaret Wilson Smith Van Patton - Aug. 13, 1929, age 69 yrs.
    5 mos.
Isaac Toll Van Patton - June 12, 1924, age 69 yrs.
William A. Smith - 1836-1891, age 55 yrs., CSA.

LOT 78
Ave. 1, Old 9
Owner - Edwin J. Mears
Ralph Mears - Sept. 9, 1884, age 3 yrs.
F. T. Mears - Sept. 7, 1896, age 53 yrs.
George Mears - Apr. 23, 1912, age 42 yrs.
Edward James Mears - (Bilisoly Blues CSA), age 84 yrs.
4 graves - no names.
General A. C. Godwin - CSA.
Charles M. Mears - July 21, 1958, age 73 yrs.
D. T. Mears - Oct. 19, 1906, age 22 yrs.
Elizabeth F. Mears - Apr. 13, 1907, age 63 yrs.
Mildred Lee Taylor - Feb. 16, 1910, age 8 days.

LOT 79
Ave. 1, Old 8
Owner - B. O'Neil, S/H
Mary W. Downing - Feb. 11, 1935, age 60 yrs.
Elizabeth Edwards - buried Oct. 26, 1885, age 75 yrs.
John Downing - Nov. 8, 1945, age 77 yrs.
Charles Downing - Oct. 14, 1958, age 55 yrs.

LOT 80
Ave. 2, Old 23

24

Owners - Francis Russ, N/H - William Boswick, S/H
South Half:
Susanna Boswick - Feb. 25, 1843, age 28 yrs. 5 mos.
Ellen R. Morgan - Oct. 21, 1894, age 57 yrs.
William D. Horgan - June 11, 1909, age 73 yrs.
North Half:
Margaret Russ - Jan. 5, 1883, age 83 yrs.
Samuel P. Russ - May 10, 1864, age 46 yrs., CSA.
Lt. F. P. Russ - CSA.
Doris May Johnson - Oct. 16, 1915.
L. M. Russ - buried Feb. 2, 1885, age 52 yrs., USN.
Thomas S. Russ - Sept. 27, 1940, age 65 yrs.
Clarence Russ - buried Feb. 2, 1885, age 20 yrs.
Margaret J. Russ - June 16, 1905, age 67 yrs.
Catherine Ellis Russ - June 16, 1909, age 4 mos.

LOT 81
Ave. 1, Old 8
Owner - J. H. Wingfield
Franklin P. Reynolds - Apr. 7, 1905, age 50 yrs.
Margaret Elizabeth and Mary Swepson - children of J. H. and
    Eliza Swepson Wingfield.
John H. Wingfield - Oct. 24, 1938, age 65 yrs.
Swepson Whitehead Wingfield - died Mar. 29, 1860, age 36 yrs.
Eliza Swepson Wingfield - June 14, 1858, age 81 yrs.
Rev. John Henry Wingfield, D.D. - Dec. 5, 1871, age 74 yrs.
Emily Ann Wingfield - 1814-1887, age 73 yrs.
Elizabeth Susan Wingfield - June 12, 1926, age 81 yrs. 9 mos.
Richard C. M. Wingfield - Oct. 15, 1890, age 52 yrs., 9th Va.
    CSA.

LOT 82
Ave. 2, Old 22
Owner - William H. Wilson
Ellen Keeling Godwin - Nov. 24, 1867, age 7 yrs.
4 graves - no names.
G. W. Godwin - buried Nov. 28, 1894, age 35 yrs.
Susan Godwin - buried Nov. 12, 1894, age 21 yrs.
A. D. B. Godwin - CSA.
Col. D. J. Godwin - buried Jan. 18, 1890, age 56 yrs., 9th Va.
    CSA.
Esther Gayle Wilson - Oct. 27, 1929, age 79 yrs. 11 mos.
Nellie Lee Wilson - buried May 31, 1898, age 38 yrs.
Richard Shane - Feb. 27, 1887, age 28 yrs.

LOT 83
Ave. 1, Old 7
Owner - Minton Walker
A. J. A.
No other names on this plot.

LOT 84
Ave. 2, Old 21
Owner - William H. Wilson
Essie Gayle Wilson - Apr. 10, 1964.
John Nelson Hodges - July 21, 1890, age 29 yrs.
William Wilson Hodges - Apr. 26, 1893, age 38 yrs.
Sarah Wilson - June 20, 1954, age 75 yrs.
William H. Wilson - age 84 yrs., Old Dominion Guard, 9th Va.
    Reg. CSA.
Esther Murdaugh Wilson - May 27, 1941, age 79 yrs.
J. W. Keeling - 9th Va. Inf. CSA.
Col. J. G. Hodges - 14th Va. Inf. CSA.
Jacob K. Wilson - Sept. 14, 1839, age 2 yrs.
Ellen W. Wilson - Apr. 18, 1811.
William H. Wilson - 1804-1880, age 75 yrs.
A. E. Wilson - buried Sept. 5, 1896, age 64 yrs., 14th Va. Regt.
    CSA.
4 graves - no names.
Annie Taylor Wilson - Oct. 5, 1909, age 77 yrs.
Arthur Taylor Wilson - Feb. 23, 1902, age 28 yrs.
Sarah Hodges - Sept. 19, 1917, age 86 yrs.

LOT 85
Old 6
Owners - Mrs. H. L. Wilson and Mrs. C. D. Burton
Sarah N. Burton - Dec. 3, 1958, age 70 yrs.
Carl D. Burton - Nov. 9, 1955, age 60 yrs.

LOT 86
Ave., 2, Old 20
Owner - John Williston
Edward, Eugenia and John Dickinson - infant children.
Sally Butt - June 19, 1849, age 57 yrs.

LOT 87
Ave. 1, Old 6
*Owners - Harding and Harrison - Transferred to Mrs. S. R.
    Moore*
Elizabeth Scarff - Apr. 6, 1888, age 87 yrs. 9 mos.

Phoebe Richards - June 11, 1910, age 86 yrs.
Harriett A. M. Warner - Nov. 24, 1890, age 55 yrs.
4 graves - no names.
A. E. McDonell - died Feb. 8, 1897, age 48 yrs., Shoemaker Bat.
   CSA.
Mrs. Ann Hargrove - Sept. 8, 1842, age 51 yrs.
G. W. R. McDonell - died Sept. 25, 1929, age 69 yrs., Grimes
   Bat.

LOT 88
Ave. 2, Old 19
Owner - Robert Stanwood
Martha S. Stanwood - Apr. 22, 1919, age 83 yrs.
Anna Stanwood - buried Apr. 8, 1886, age 71 yrs.
Martha Ann Stanwood - Mar. 15, 1841, child.
Robert Stanwood - Nov. 2, 1841, age 43 yrs.
Julian Whitehead - Apr. 5, 1888, age 1 mo.
6 graves - no names.
Samuel James Stanwood - died July 15, 1936, age 79 yrs., Mach
   Mate 1 Class USN.
Samuel Stanwood - Sept. 11, 1855, age 46 yrs.
Mrs. Sophia Shannon - Apr. 12, 1854, age 63 yrs.
Cora Stanwood Darden - 1869-1935, age 65 yrs.
Martha Stanwood - Sept. 24, 1844, age 25 yrs.
Elizabeth Virginia Stanwood - Feb. 15, 1812.

LOT 89
Ave. 1, Old 5
Owners - Simon Ghio and Dickerson
Silas Powers - buried June 16, 1886, age 93 yrs.
Rodman G. Savage - Jan. 8, 1895, age 7 mos.

LOT 90
Ave. 2, Old 18
Owner - J. L. Porter
Alice F. Ellison Porter - Nov. 9, 1889, age 49 yrs.
John L. Porter - Dec. 14, 1893, age 79 yrs., Constructor CSN.
Susan N. Porter - 1817-1903, age 85 yrs.
George H. Ellison - 1873-1873.
Lt. William Porter - 12th Va. Mil. Inf. Rev. War.
Elizabeth Porter - 1764-1846.
Fannie Porter - June 8, 1843, age 54 yrs.

LOT 91
Ave. 1, Old 4

Owner - Joseph Reynolds
Martha Reynolds - July 12, 1838, age 39 yrs.
George Reynolds - July 9, 1838, age 6 wks.
James Collins - Mar. 9, 1851, age 15 yrs.
Joseph Reynolds - Mar. 19, 1876, age 73 yrs.
Samuel D. Reynolds - Nov. 10, 1855, age 22 yrs.

LOT 92
Ave. 2, Old 18
Owner - W. N. White, S/H
Archur W. Sturtevant - buried June 17, 1892, age 2 mos. 13
    days.
William Andrews Wright - died Apr. 25, 1887, age 2 yrs.
John C. Morrisett - Mar. 1, 1934, age 38 yrs.
M. B. Sturtevant - buried Nov. 8, 1895, age 59 yrs.
Capt. William F. White - Dec. 24, 1872, age 41 yrs., 6th Va. Inf.
    CSA.
1 grave - no name.
Roselie White - died June 30, 1861, age 19 yrs.
Joshua White - July 9, 1870, age 62 yrs.
Mrs. Elizabeth M. White - Dec. 1, 1874, age 75 yrs.

LOT 93
Ave. 1, Old 4
Owner - Samuel Turner, S/H
Jeannette H. Turner - Nov. 5, 1872, age 64 yrs.
Samuel Turner - June 25, 1881, age 80 yrs.
Charles R. Turner - Apr. 21, 1895, age 48 yrs.
Samuel Boyd - Sept. 18, 1896, age 48 yrs.
Mary E. Boyd - Nov. 11, 1875, age 32 yrs.

LOT 94
Ave. 2, Old 17
Owners - Hoops and Brown, N/H
5 graves - no names.
William T. Robinson - Apr. 16, 1910, age 69 yrs.
Joseph M. Robinson - Dec. 18, 1916, age 46 yrs.
Mary J. Robinson - Aug. 31, 1930, age 64 yrs.
Anna A. Robinson - May 7, 1921, age 78 yrs.
Sarah Wakefield - June 8, 1913, age 87 yrs.

LOT 95
Ave. 1, Old 3
Owner - Thomas J. Hobday, N/H

Thomas J. Hobday - Sept. 10, 1885, age 61 yrs.
Mother
Sister

LOT 96
Ave. 2, Old 17
Owners - Hoops and Brown, S/H
Aletha W. Robinson - Dec. 1, 1944, age 77 yrs.
William T. Robinson - May 23, 1955, age 79 yrs.
Mildred T. Robinson - Oct. 13, 1944, age 70 yrs.
2 graves - no names.
Boush child - stillborn, buried June 1, 1884.

LOT 97
Ave. 1, Old 3
Owner - Julia Armistead, S/H
John H. Blamire - buried Oct. 30, 1894, age 5 yrs. 10 mos.
Julia C. Swann - Apr. 30, 1843, age 46 yrs.
Mrs. Julia Armistead - Aug. 6, 1857, age 81 yrs.

LOT 98
Ave. 2, Old 16
Owner - John Linn
John Linn, Sr. - Sept. 19, 1843, age 45 yrs.
Eliza Linn - June 22, 1880, age 78 yrs.
James Linn - Apr. 29, 1855, age 30 yrs.
William Linn - Dec. 21, 1880, age 50 yrs.
C. B. Linn - CSA.
10 graves - no names.
Frank P. Johnson - buried May 26, 1896, age 45 yrs.
Alice V. Johnson - Feb. 24, 1901, age 45 yrs.
Mary E. Johnson - Jan. 24, 1911, age 62 yrs.
Thomas Johnson - Sept. 17, 1854, age 39 yrs.
Ellen Lash - Sept. 2, 1883, age 57 yrs.
Charles B. Linn - Mar. 13, 1887, age 80 yrs.

LOT 99
Ave. 1, Old 2
*Owners - William H. Wilson - Changed May 13, 1947, to Frank
Nash Bilisoly, Jr.*
Charlotte Langhorne - Oct. 7, 1879, age 84 yrs.
Mrs. Nancy Wilson - Jan. 26, 1840, age 75 yrs.
William Wilson - July 19, 1838, age 77 yrs.
body - brick grave.
Maurice B. Langhorne - Aug. 27, 1851, age 36 yrs.

Frank Nash Bilisoly - Jan. 22, 1983 (vault).
Emily B. B. Wilson - Aug. 12, 1855, age 41 yrs.

LOT 100
Ave. 2, Old 15
Owner - Barnett, N/H
2 graves - no names.
Elizabeth Barnard - buried Aug. 28, 1890, age 49 yrs.

LOT 101
Ave. 1, Old 1
Owner - Dr. Thomas Williamson
Jennie Kerns Williamson - Dec. 11, 1935, age 72 yrs. 9 mos.
Thomas W. Wysham - buried Jan. 14, 1892, age 22 yrs.
Clarence Henning Williamson - Mar. 12, 1911, age 65 yrs.,
    N.L.A. Blues CSA.
Dr. James Williamson - Apr. 1, 1871, age 41 yrs.
T. Harrison Williamson - June 21, 1873, age 35 yrs.
Caroline Cornelia Williamson - May 18, 1914, age 71 yrs.
3 graves - no names.
Caroline A. Williamson - July 4, 1885, age 78 yrs.
Dr. Thomas Williamson - died Jan. 12, 1859, age 68 yrs., Sur-
    geon USN.
Charles H. Williamson, M.D. - died Sept. 10, 1894, age 68 yrs.,
    Surgeon CSN.
Emily Williamson - Jan. 28, 1856, age 24 yrs.
Williamson child - May 30, 188-.

LOT 102
Ave 2, Old 15, S/H
Eugenia H. Fraetas - Nov. 17, 1850, age 3 yrs. 1 mo.
1 grave - no name.
Mary Ann H. Fraetas - Nov. 7, 1853, age 25 yrs. 5 mos.
Roselie A. Williams - July 9, 1860, age 28 yrs.
Lory Ann B. Fraetas - Jan. 30, 1852, age 12 mos.

LOT 103
Old 19
Owners - Carey and Burroughs
Cecil M. Burroughs - buried Aug. 20, 1888, age 1 day.
Blanch Broughton - Mar. 31, 1953, age 72 yrs.
George Atwell Broughton - Mar. 4, 1967 (vault).
Mary A. Burroughs - Nov. 14, 1920, age 63 yrs.
Richard B. Burroughs - Feb. 18, 1911, age 54 yrs.
Kendall James Brennan - Sept. 12, 1970 (vault).

Mary V. Carey - Dec. 30, 1892, age 59 yrs.
Arthur E. Carey - Sept. 21, 1868, age 8 yrs.
James W. Carey - Jan. 16, 1905, age 71 yrs.
Richard A. Burroughs - died Aug. 21, 1910, age 5 yrs., moved to
  Norfolk, Forrest Lawn, June 12, 1947.
Elgar Murphy - Jan. 29, 1904, moved to Oak Grove Sept. 11,
  1970.

LOT 104
Ave. 3, Old 18
Owner - C. R. Robertson
Harry Robertson Gray - 1889-1934, age 44 yrs.
Angelia Robertson Gray - Mar. 25, 1982 (vault).
Charles R. Robertson - Dec. 18, 1931, age 78 yrs.
Anna Amelia Robertson - Nov. 17, 1939, age 86 yrs.
Tilton G. Robertson - Nov. 5, 1917, age 22 yrs.
Edward T. Robertson - Feb. 23, 1881, age 5 yrs.
Charles M. Robertson - Nov. 14, 1886, age 8 yrs.
Thomas M. Robertson - Dec. 6, 1891, age 4 yrs. 9 mos.

LOT 105
Ave. 2, Old 20
Owner - W. H. Stokes, N/H
Josephine Clemm Stokes - May 8, 1905, age 56 yrs.
William H. Stokes - Dec. 15, 1902, age 57 yrs.
Emily J. Stokes - Aug. 10, 1902, age 50 yrs.
Josie Stokes - Aug. 3, 1885.
Willie Stokes - June 22, 1885, age 1 yr.
Emilie Stokes Good (or Goad) - 1886-1934, age 46 yrs.
Irene Daugherty Stokes - buried Oct. 24, 1962.
Ralph Morton Stokes, Sr. - buried Dec. 30, 1974.

LOT 106
Ave. 3, Old 17
Owners - Virginia Boush, S/H - Thomas C. Goode, N/H
South Half:
J. E. Boush - buried May 25, 1885, age 62 yrs.
George W. Boush - Apr. 20, 1892, age 20 yrs.
C. R. Boush - Oct. 15, 1896, age 45 yrs.
Genevieve Boush - Apr. 25, 1938, age 79 yrs.
Brick covered grave - no name.
Slab on name.
North Half:
Emma Jane Etheredge - Jan. 2, 1915, age 77 yrs.
Alexander E. Etheredge - June 16, 1909, age 79 yrs.

Fanny Goode - July 9, 1946, age 86 yrs.
Thomas Cambell Goode - May 22, 1908, age 50 yrs.

LOT 107
Ave. 2, Old 20
Owner - Thomas L. Rice, S/H
Almira V. Rice - July 21, 1956, age 93 yrs.
2 graves - no names.
Mary Etta Rice - May 30, 1885, age 28 yrs.
Edward M. Rice - buried Mar. 28, 1889, age 7 yrs. 7 mos.
Oscar Perkins - 1889-1933, July 15, 1933, age 43 yrs.
Rebecca L. Perkins - June 8, 1977 (vault).

LOT 108
Ave. 3, Old 16
Owner - George C. White
Chase Wells Morgan - Sept. 26, 1917, age 33 yrs. 5 mos.
Mary Elizabeth Morgan - buried June 3, 1963.
George Edward White, Jr. - Dec. 28, 1979.
Annie Elizabeth White - Nov. 19, 1966, age 77 yrs.
George E. White - Apr. 5, 1947, age 76 yrs.
Mary E. White - age 4 mos.
Minnie Laurence White - Aug. 30, 1904, age 26 yrs.
Thomas Howard White - Feb. 20, 1906, age 38 yrs.
Mary Elizabeth White - Oct. 27, 1904, age 58 yrs.
George C. White - buried Sept. 14, 1891, age 52 yrs.

LOT 109
Ave. 2, Old 21
Owner - William N. Nash, N/H
Dora White - Mar. 7, 1892, age 30 yrs.
William N. White - Dec. 21, 1917, age 59 yrs.
Ruth Hutching White - May 30, 1922, age 50 yrs.
Maranda White - Feb. 10, 1889, age 48 yrs.
Mary E. White - buried Feb. 11, 188-, age 60 yrs.

LOT 110
Ave. 2, Old 21
Owner - J. F. Carr, S/H
4 graves - no names.
Monument
Lee Godwin - buried Apr. 21, 188-, age 3 yrs. 2 mos.
James F. Carr - Jan. 1, 1912, age 83 yrs.
Elvira W. Carr - Mar. 15, 1915, age 82 yrs.
Nellie Elizabeth Carr - Feb. 19, 1931, age 70 yrs.

Murdaugh - stillborn, buried Oct. 1, 1890.
Martha A. Bingham - buried June 2, 1888, age 75 yrs.

LOT 111
Ave. 2, Old 22
Owner - G. T. Minton
Orville F. Minton - Dec. 7, 1894, age 29 yrs.
Thomas H. Minton - 1878-1909, Jan. 6th, age 30 yrs.
Martha Ellen Minton - June 19, 1902, age 43 yrs.
Lucy Minton - Nov. 7, 1887, age 1 yr.
Thomas Giles Minton - July 19, 1929, age 73 yrs.
Margaret F. Minton - June 21, 1892, age 65 yrs.
Giles T. Minton - Dec. 16, 1894, age 67 yrs.

LOT 112
Ave. 3, Old 15
Owner - William C. White
James Turner White - June 15, 1909, age 57 yrs.
Sarah Wilson White - Jan. 18, 1029, age 75 yrs.
William White, M.D. - Jan. 22, 1894, age 75 yrs., CSA.
Henrietta K. White - Jan. 7, 1890, age 63 yrs.

LOT 113
Ave. 2, Old 23
Owner - H. C. Hudgins
John Ellsworth Rapelye - May 15, 1962, age 83 yrs.
S. Legrand - buried Mar. 12, 1896, age 12 yrs.
Nannie L. Hudgins Rapelye - Sept. 10, 1964.
Lucrece P. Langhorne Hudgins - Sept. 10, 1903, age 55 yrs.
Henry Clay Hudgins - Aug. 6, 1913, age 71 yrs.
J. Bilisoly Hudgins - June 11, 1958, age 77 yrs.
Emma M. Hudgins - Dec. 11 1968 (vault).
Mabel Brown Hudgins - Sept. 22, 1966.
Augustus Kussuth Hudgins - June 12, 1883.
Maurice Hudgins - Sept. 3, 1947, age 73 yrs.
Fitzhugh Lee Hudgins - Mar. 27, 1958, age 72 yrs.
Elizabeth Wingfield Hudgins - Oct. 9, 1894, age 4 yrs.
Minnie E. Hudgins - June 29, 1889, age 19 yrs.
Sallie Frances Hudgins - Jan. 17, 1943, age 87 yrs.

LOT 114
Ave. 3, Old 14
Owners - M. A. Riddick, N/H - Langhorne, S/H
North Half:
Legh W. Riddick - Apr. 15, 1977 (vault).

Mat Legh Riddick - July, 14, 1967 (vault).
William Maurice Riddick - 1868-1934, age 66 yrs.
Capt. J. W. Riddick - Sept. 22, 1869, age 26 yrs., CSA.
Mary Anna Riddick - 1847-1934, age 87 yrs.
Annie
South Half:
W. S. Langhorne - Jan. 7, 1910, age 64 yrs., CSA.
Rosalie Langhorne - Mar. 16, 1907, age 56 yrs.
Lulie E. Langhorne - May 31, 1888, age 14 yrs. 7 mos.

LOT 115
Ave. 2, Old 24
Owner - D. W. Todd, Jr.
James G. Todd - Jan. 27, 1946, age 71 yrs.
Ethel Herbert Todd - Sept. 21, 1969 (vault).
Ida T. Foster - Oct. 22, 1950, age 81 yrs.
Annis Gill Todd - Apr. 10, 1916, age 73 yrs.
Darius Webb Todd - Nov. 19, 1919, age 83 yrs.
Todd - stillborn, Nov. 26, 1908.

LOT 116
Ave. 3, Old 13
Owner - William A. Davis
Blanks Herbert Davis - buried July 14, 1971.
Effie Lambert Davis - buried May 13, 1966.
William A. Davis - died June 13, 1912, age 74 yrs.
Mary Ann Davis - Apr. 5, 1926, age 87 yrs.
Mary Arlene Mattox - Feb. 19, 1956, age 32 yrs.
Helen Davis Wonycott - Dec. 25, 1898, age 6 yrs.
Lillian Davis Wonycott - Feb. 26, 1894, age 24 yrs.
Mary Beulah Davis - Jan. 31, 1895, age 17 yrs.

LOT 117
Ave. 2, Old R1
Owners - Gill and Todd
Franklin David Gill - July 16, 1913, age 55 yrs.
Cora Mapp Gill - Aug. 3, 1959, age 88 yrs.
James Richard Gill - Mar. 8, 1930, age 30 yrs.
Margaret C. Todd - Nov. 27, 1884, age 3 1/2 days.
Will C. Gill - June 12, 1945, age 40 yrs.
Agnes Gill - buried Dec. 17, 1894, age 17 yrs.
Gill - stillborn of F. D. and M. F. Gill, Feb. 1, 1888.
Mollie F. Gill - Feb. 6, 1888, age 26 yrs.
Franklin Daird Gill, Jr. - Aug. 22, 1910, age 14 yrs.

Agnes C. Gill - 1816-1889, age 73 yrs.
David Gill - 1810-1875, age 64 yrs.

LOT 118
Old 103
Owner - Thomas L. Wilkins
Linwood Thomas Wilkins - Jan. 5, 1928, age 23 yrs.
Ethel Eloise Wilkins - Aug. 15, 1918-Aug. 16, 1927.
Baby Wilkins - Aug. 27, 1950.
3 graves - no names.
Gatsy T. Wilkins - June 26, 1958, age 75 yrs.
Whitmeal Wilkins - Mar. 19, 1931, age 74 yrs.
Ethel E. Wilkins - May 16, 1927, age 8 yrs.
Mary F. Wilkins - Mar. 28, 1899, age 45 yrs. (removed to Olive
    Branch Cemetery June 28, 1958).
Hugwod - stillborn, Nov. 22, 1928.
Taylor - stillborn of William A. and Sadie Taylor, Apr. 6, 1909.

LOT 119
Ave. 3, Old Q1
Owner - John H. Stout
John Imlay Stout - 1857-1871, age 13 yrs.
John H. Stout - age 82 yrs., Quarter Master CSA.
Mary F. Stout - 1910, age 82 yrs.
Eliza Stout - Sept. 7, 1946, age 86 yrs.
Isabella Stout Barlow - Nov. 22, 1907, age 40 yrs.
Mrs. Abigail K. Staples - June 12, 1888, age 83 yrs.
Sarah C. Manning - June 5, 1904, age 63 yrs.
Virginia S. Staples - Aug. 9, 1910, age 67 yrs.
Joseph G. Stout - 1915.
Jennette W. Stout - Dec. 4, 1909, age 57 yrs.

LOT 120
Ave. 2, Old 214
Owner - Patrick Williams
Brick-covered grave - no name.
2 slabs - no names.
3 vacant.
1 grave - no name.
Laura W. Riggan - Jan. 20, 1954, age 63 yrs.
John R. Riggan - Nov. 4, 1959, age 81 yrs.
Margaret Williams Bogg - Jan. 14, 1984 (vault).
Chesley Roy Boggs - Jan. 29, 1968, age 72 yrs. (vault).
Gin Pat Williams - buried July 21, 1884, age 56 yrs.
Annie C. Williams - July 21, 1932, age 64 yrs.

James P. Williams - Apr. 3, 1913, age 52 yrs.
John Royal Riggan - Jan. 2, 1934, age 22 yrs.
Marion R. Williamson - March 22, 1902, age 39 yrs.
George R. Williams - buried June 12, 1891, age 1 mo.
Earnest N. Woolman - Aug. 12, 1899, age 1 yr. 8 mos.

LOT 121
Ave. 3, Old 216
Owner - George W. Grice
Monument
Laurence - stillborn, May 25, 1923.
George W. Grice, Jr. - Dec. 25, 1880, age 8 yrs.
Margaret Nash Grice - Jan. 10, 1864, age 33 yrs.
Maj. George W. Grice - Nov. 12, 1875, age 51 yrs., V. M. Dept.
  CSA.
Hennie H. Grice - June 9, 1917, age 77 yrs.
Hennie Grice - Jan. 2, 1867.
Georgette Grice - July 23, 1850, age 3 yrs.
Charles Martin Clark - Jan. 27, 1856, 3 yrs. 6 mos.
George Grice Clark - June 7, 1861, age 3 yrs.
Cornelia Grice - Oct. 19, 1945, age 70 yrs.
George Grice Stout - Mar. 18, 1870, age 8 yrs.
Dr. Joseph Grice - Oct. 21, 1947, age 78 yrs.

LOT 122
Old 213
Owner - J. E. Deans, N/H
Elvira White Simmons - buried Nov. 14, 1884, age 79 yrs.
Alice Deans - Jan. 10, 1913, age 60 yrs.
Eliza M. Deans - Jan. 21, 1912, age 55 yrs.
Ada Deans - July 14, 1858, age 5 mos.
Marshall Brigg Deans - 4 yrs.
Capt. J. E. Deans - buried May 10, 1895, age 66 yrs. 4 mos.,
  CSA.
Martha A. Deans - 1832-1912, age 80 yrs.
Edwin Deans - 1853-1883, age 30 yrs.

LOT 123
Ave. 2, Old 213
Owner - Henry Lindsay
Mary Ann Lindsay - 1824-1908, age 83 yrs.
Henry Lindsay - 1822-1903, age 81 yrs.
Rachel Lindsay - Apr. 17, 1853, age 62 yrs.

Edward Laurence - Sept. 10, 1855, age 22 yrs.
1 grave - no name.
Eliza Story - buried Nov. 26, 1889, age 79 yrs.

LOT 124
Ave. 3, Old 215
Owner - George Brent
William J. Brent - 1860-1937, age 76 yrs., Carpenter's Mate
   USN Spanish American War.
7 graves - no names.
C. F. Craft - buried May 1, 1883, age 6 days.
Matthew child - 1884.
John F. Brent - Jan. 3, 1908, age 73 yrs.
Herbert Matthews - buried Sept. 2, 1885, age 5 mos.
Lelie Craft - Feb. 2, 1892, age 3 yrs. 7 mos.
Ruth L. Craft - buried July 16, 1894, age 1 yr. 7 mos.
Mary B. Brent - buried July 26, 189-, age 34 yrs.
Sarah E. Brent - buried May 7, 1895, age 48 yrs.
Eliza Ann Brent - Feb. 6, 1905, age 68 yrs.
Charles F. Craft - Oct. 29, 1924, age 72 yrs.
Susie Brent Craft - Jan. 2, 1930, age 79 yrs.
George M. Brent - July 15, 1909, age 86 yrs.

LOT 125
Ave. 2, Old 218
Owners - C. W. Harvey and Joseph Hobday
Ann E. Harvey - May 31, 1887, age 75 yrs.
Virginius Harvey - Nov. 25, 1912, age 64 yrs.
A. W. Harvey - age 45 yrs. 10 mos., 9th Va. Inf. CSA.
W. Harvey - 9th Va. CSA.
4 graves - no names.
Florence Stone Harvey - Sept. 21, 1905, age 52 yrs.
Mrs. Ida Howard Hobday - May 28, 1939, age 79 yrs.
Joseph G. Hobday - Apr. 2, 1897, age 39 yrs.
Capt. J. Hobday - CSA.
John E. Hobday - July 9, 1916.

LOT 126
Ave. 3, Old 217
Owner - W. D. Young
Julia A. Smith - Mar. 1, 1913, age 34 yrs.
Margaret Ann Godwin - buried May 14, 1888, Washington, D.C.

LOT 127
Ave. 2, Old 219

Owner - John N. Ashton
John C. Ashton - Sept. 17, 1918, age 3 yrs.
Clara McKensie - Apr. 4, 1933, age 51 yrs.
Charles Burditt Ashton - Dec. 5, 1913, age 65 yrs.
Richard Newton Ashton - died Apr. 6, 1911, age 64 yrs., 5th Va.
  Calv. CSA.
Mrs. Ellen V. M. Cabell - Sept. 2, 1904, age 52 yrs.
Ellen Theodosia Ashton - Feb. 16, 1891, age 69 yrs.
John Newton Ashton - Aug. 13, 1874, age 59 yrs.
John Newton Ashton - Aug. 20, 1855, age 71 yrs.
Henry William McKenzie - 1876-1939.
Clara Maupin Ashton McKenzie - 1881-1933.
Martha C. Ashton - June 14, 1947.
J. Edgar Ashton - 1839-1882, N.L. A.B., CSA.

LOT 128
Old 220
Owners - John Borum and Brothers
John E. Borum - Apr. 27, 1919, age 66 yrs.
Charles Carlton Ricketts - Sept. 8, 1939, age 34 yrs.
James E. Ricketts - Nov. 14, 1950, 83 yrs.
Elizabeth Ricketts - Nov. 26, 1957, 85 yrs.
John L. Borum - Mar. 25, 1918, 80 yrs.
Sarah F. Borum - Jan. 29, 1906, 69 yrs.
Gracie V. Ricketts - Dec. 14, 1903, 1 yr. 2 mos.
1 grave - no name.
James E. Ricketts - Dec. 12, 1897, 7 yrs. 3 mos.
Reserved - one grave for John A. Ricketts, grandson of John B.
  Borum.

LOT 129
Ave. 2, Old 196
Owner - David Bain
William W. Bain - 1853-1932, age 79 yrs.
Rosa L. Bain - Jan. 3, 1926, age 71 yrs.
Fannie Webb Roy - Feb. 18, 1907, age 56 yrs.
1 grave - no name.
Sarah Elsie Nash - Reserved for her.
Thomas E. Nash - Oct. 11, 1914, age 55 yrs.
Wilder W. Nash - June 1, 1892, age 1 yr. 23 days.
Mrs. Ellen Watts Nash - Oct. 29, 1945, age 74 yrs.
David L. Watts - May 22, 1895, age 1 yrs.

LOT 130
Ave. 3, Old 221

Owner - Francis C. Herbert
Lewis Day Armistead - buried June 16, 1888, age 6 mos.
Herbert B. Armistead - June 28, 1888, age 6 mos.
Francis C. Herbert - 1807-1872.
5 graves - no names.
Mary E. Herbert - 1816-1855.
Sarah E. Herbert Faison - Feb. 15, 1890, age 42 yrs.
Hattie M. Faison - buried Mar. 5, 189-, age 8 yrs.
Jennie Ruth Faison - May 25, 1900, 3 yrs. 6 mos.
Frank D. Faison - buried May 3, 1894, age 20 yrs.

LOT 131
Ave. 2, Old 5
Owner - Dr. James L. Hatton
Mildred May Martin - Mar. 9, 1902, age 8 mos.
Reserved for Mrs. Riddick.
Caroline Leckie Hatton Nash - 1860-1922, age 62 yrs.
Edgar Nash - 1855-1925, age 70 yrs.
Joseph Moore Hatton - 1862-1922, age 60 yrs.
Jogn G. Hatton - 1858-1919, age 64 yrs.
Stonewall Benson Nash - Jan. 24, 1939, age 74 yrs.
Emmeline Watts Hatton - 1865-1931, age 65 yrs.
Alexander Eccles Nash - 1896-1897, age 1 yr. 4 mos.
Jeanette Nash - 1892-1894, age 1 yr. 2 mos.
Olivia J. Hatton - 1833-1911, age 78 yrs.
Dr. James L. Hatton - 1831-1893, age 61 yrs.

LOT 132
Ave. 3, Old L
Owner - Strangers Section
Isaac Evebtsen - May 25, 1838, age 37 yrs.
James Crookshank Hanks - Oct. 28, 1832, age 28 yrs.
W. H. Crittenden - Aug. 7, 1842, age 23 yrs.
Thedore H. Stanley - of North Carolina, Dec. 30, 1875, age 31
    yrs.
John Middleton - Apr. 12, 1833, age 21 yrs., Midshipman USS
    Java.
Jan Elizabeth Parker - Sept. 16, 1832, age 8 yrs.
Andrew J. McFaddin - July 27, 1855, age 31 yrs.
Eliza Murray - of Alexandria, D.C., July 18, 1835, age 25 yrs.
Joseph Pruden - Sept. 9, 1847, age 24 yrs.
Frederick Pate - June 1, 1846, age 23 yrs.

LOT 133
2nd Ave., Old G

Owner - N. B. Ridley
Louise Blunt Drewry - 1844-1916, age 71 yrs.
Julia Maclin Goodwin - Nov. 8, 1926, age 72 yrs.
Elizabeth R. Baggett - Mar. 27, 1951, age 66 yrs.
Francis Baggett - Mar. 16, 1952, age 64 yrs.
Nettie Godwin Ridley - Oct. 5, 1961, age 84 yrs.
Francis Thomas Ridley, M.D. - 1881-1934, age 52 yrs.
Annie Blount Ridley - Apr. 6, 1979 (vault).
Anna Field Ridley - 1849-1924, age 75 yrs.
Norfleet Blunt Ridley - 1848-1893, age 45 yrs.
William G. Ridley - 1877-1916, age 38 yrs.
Robert Ridley - Apr. 10, 1933, age 58 yrs.

LOT 134
Ave. 3, Old K
Owner - Mrs. Charles R. Nash
Rebecca Nash - Apr. 12, 1941, age 84 yrs.
Charles Reid Nash - Apr. 11, 1918, age 68 yrs.
James Spaulding-Murdock - Apr. 3, 1920, age 39 yrs., Commander USN.
Rebecca Murdock - Feb. 19, 1961, age 81 yrs.
Mary Byrd Marshall Nash - Jan. 25, 1905, age 7 yrs.

LOT 135
Ave. 2, Old F2
Owner - L. W. Howlett
Aracana Tatem - Aug. 6, 1923, age 72 yrs.
Charles Tatem - June 23, 1908, age 12 yrs.
Paul Anderton Tatem - Mar. 21, 1934, age 52 yrs.
2 graves - no names.
Mary Lucrece Howlett - Mar. 6, 1935, age 85 yrs. 9 mos.
Warner L. Howlett - June 2, 1894, age 70 yrs.
George Nathaniel Howlett - Dec. 2, 1938, age 69 yrs.
Mary Lou Howlett - Nov. 3, 1878, age 5 yrs.
R. Fanny Tatem - July 31, 1878, age 49 yrs.
Virginia Tatem - age 6 mos.
Aracana Tatem - Aug. 6, 1923, age 72 yrs.
Charles M. Tatem - June 23, 1908, age 12 yrs.
Paul Anderton Tatem - Mar. 21, 1934, age 52 yrs.

LOT 136
Ave. 3, Old J
Owners - Confederate Soldiers and Stonewall Camp
Confederate Veterans and The Sisters of Mercy
George C. King - buried Mar. 22, 1886, age 8 yrs.

Clarence King - Apr. 14, 1886, age 17 yrs.
Annie F. King - buried Apr. 14, 1886, age 15 yrs.
Mary V. King - buried Apr. 20, 1886, age 19 yrs.
Elizabeth W. Taylor - Jan. 13, 1935, age 75 yrs.
J. R. Hughes - CSA from Petersburg, Va.
David Kantz - CSA Valley of Va.
Albert Johnson - CSA Isle of Wight Co., Va.
Charles E. Smith - died May 8, 1861, Co. 1, 4th Regt. Ga. Vol.
    CSA, Macon, Ga.
Young H. Smith - died May 11, 1861, Co. 1, 4th Regt. Ga. Vol.
    CSA, Macon, Ga.
Unknown Soldier - from Ga., CSA.
Elizabeth Butt - Aug. 28, 1875, age 70 yrs.

LOT 137
Ave. 2, Old F1
Owner - B. H. Owens
Virginia Owens Royall - July 29, 1944, age 66 yrs.
Leslie J. Royall - Sept. 28, 1962.
Ruth Owens Dickerson - June 3, 1937, age 64 yrs.
Leslie John Royall, Jr.
Benjamin Harris Owens, Jr. - 1879-1904, age 24 yrs.
Missouri S. Owens - 1839-1911, age 71 yrs.
Benjamin H. Owens - 1830-1902, age 71 yrs., CSA
1 grave - no name.

LOT 138
Ave. 3, Old J
Owner - John S. Stubbs
Robert Armistead Stubbs - Dec. 7, 1868, age 79 yrs.
Stella H. Stubbs - Feb. 21, 1865, age 56 yrs.
John S. Stubbs - Feb. 19, 1884, age 72 yrs.
Annie W. Stewart - Nov. 28, 1883, age 35 yrs.

LOT 139
Ave. 2, Old 41
Owner - A. B. Smith
Anna Marie Smith - Aug. 5, 1838, age 30 yrs.
Anna M. Smith - Aug. 6, 1838, age 3 mos.
Nannie E. Smith - Dec. 20, 1928, age 77 yrs.
Jane E. Smith - Dec. 1, 1892, age 81 yrs.
Dr. Arthur B. Smith - Sept. 16, 1865, age 60 yrs.
Edward L. Smith - Dec. 22, 1859, age 25 yrs.
Charles R. Smith - 1853-1855.
Elizabeth B. Smith - 1845-1846.

Arthur Smith - Sept. 9, 1867, age 27.
James Edward Smith - Sept. 20, 1867, age 21 yrs.
Ann Bruce Smith - Mar. 27, 1940, age 89 yrs.
Jack Quarles Hewlett Smith - Nov. 22, 1910, age 62 yrs.
May Bruce Russell - Nov. 13, 1951, age 72 yrs.
Indiana Smith - Dec. 20, 1910, age 80 yrs.
Jack Smith - Aug. 17, 1942, age 60 yrs.
Mary L. Baugham - Jan. 15, 1911, age 75 yrs.

LOT 140
Ave. 3, Old 55
Owners - Curlin and Etheridge, N/H
Aunt Kessiz Miller - no date in book after 1859.
Elizabeth Etheridge, my mother - between 1852 and 1855.
Joshua Etheridge, my father - July 18, 1852, age 55 yrs.
Susan Fenn, my sister - between 1840 and 1850.
G.E.F.

LOT 141
Ave. 3, Old 55
Owners - Curlin and Etheridge, S/H
Nellie Calvert - May 1, 1892.
Ruth E. Calvert - Apr. 4, 1894, age 5 1/2 mos.
Mable C. Calvert - buried Feb. 2, 1895, age 12 hrs.
James W. Spring - Apr. 10, 1898, age 34 yrs.
Paul Swen White - buried Aug. 6, 1886, age 2 yrs.
Mary E. Spring - buried July 27, 1888, age 15 yrs. 6 mos.
Louisanna Taylor - buried Aug. 7, 1890, age 42 yrs.
Laura P. Thayer - Nov. 23, 1908, age 83 yrs.

LOT 142
Ave. 3, Old 54
Owner - William E. Roy
William Whitson, Sr. - Apr. 4, 1890, age 48 yrs.
Mary A. Nicholson - July 6, 1901, age 50 yrs.
Milton W. Yoke - Feb. 21, 1902, age 1 day.
Addie Nicholson - Apr. 7, 1922, age 80 yrs.
Wade H. Whitson, Jr. - May 3, 1916, age 1 yr. 14 days.
William E. Roy - May 30, 1842, age 77 yrs.
Nancy Ann Roy - Sept. 20, 1855, age 82 yrs.
Ellismer Skeeter - May 12, 1873, age 6 mos.
Elizabeth J. Skeeter - Dec. 13, 1872, age 33 yrs. 6 mos.
Michale Whitson - Aug. 17, 1862, age 51 yrs.

LOT 143
Ave. 2, Old 40
Owner - Robert Tatem
Dinah Clark - June 1852.
Robert Herbert Tatem - 1838-1917, age 79 yrs.
2 graves - no names.
Mary Ann Tatem - Aug. 6, 1884, age 76 yrs.
Robert H. Tatem - Mar. 26, 1849, age 50 yrs.
Cary Baxton Tatem - Aug. 18, 1934, age 83 yrs.
Virginia Tatem - buried July 16, 1897, age 5 yrs. 5 mos.
Kate Davenport Campbell - Mar. 28, 1856, age 13 mos.
Charles C. Tatem - Aug. 28, 1855, age 14 yrs.
Charles Clark - Aug. 1855.
John Anne Tatem - July 20, 1931, age 73 yrs.

LOT 144
Ave. 3, Old 53
Owner - Elias Bridges
Franklin P. Jarvis - June 17, 1905, age 6 mos.
Virginia D. Jarvis - buried Aug. 9, 1892, age 10 mos.
Frank Jarvis - buried June 14, 1895, age 9 mos.
Bussel May Jarvis - June 19, 1903, age 1 yr. 1 mo.
Ethel Garland Jarvis - June 20, 1899, age 6 mos.
William F. Jarvis - buried June 16, 1897, age 1 yr. 2 mos.
James A. Bridges
Mary F. Bridges
Mary Ann Bridges - May 12, 1885, age 6 yrs. 3 mos.
Elias Gregory Bridges - Apr. 2, 1886, age 39 yrs.
William W. Bridges - Apr. 12, 1861, age 17 yrs.
Mary Ann Bridges - Dec. 30, 1884, age 76 yrs.
Elias G. Bridges - Jan. 8, 1890, age 82 yrs.
Thomas W. Bridges - Oct. 15, 1907, age 69 yrs., CSN.
Ann Eskridge Jarvis - Dec. 18, 1900, age 67 yrs.
William Jarvis - Aug. 23, 1899, age 71 years.

LOT 145
Ave. 2, Old 39
Owner - J. B. Emmerson
Monument to Confederates erected by John H. Lewis.
Emmerson, father - 1859, age 44 yrs.
Julia B. Whitehead - buried July 23, 1897, age 3 yrs.
George W. Emmerson - June 27, 1901, age 57 yrs., Co. G, 9th
    Va. Inf. CSA.
Susan A. Emmerson - Sept. 28, 1855, age 39 yrs.

James B. Emmerson - Jan. 5, 1856, age 53 yrs.
Sarah N. Emmerson - Oct. 2, 1855, age 45 yrs.

LOT 146
Ave. 3, Old 52
Owner - John J. Land
John J. Land - Jan. 5, 1842, age 29 yrs.
Eliza F. Land Wilson - Aug. 28, 1892, age 72 yrs.
John J. Land - May 6, 1858, age 18 yrs.
Sarah E. Land - Dec. 4, 1925, age 88 yrs.

LOT 147
Ave. 2, Old 38
Owner - Trinity Church
7 graves - no names.
Walter Ellis - Oct. 6, 1930, age 51 yrs.
Isaac R. Fagerland - Feb. 5, 1916, age 71 yrs.
Mollie Ann White - Apr. 10, 1934, age 64 yrs.
Henry A. Totley - Aug. 27, 1927, age 67 yrs.
Rev. J. Howard Veazey - June 27, 1888, age 35 yrs. 8 mos.
Julia A. Murray - June 15, 1908, age 79 yrs.
Bessie B. Wright - buried Jan. 25, 1897, age 20 yrs.
George Emmiett Taylor - June 7, 1900, age 9 mos.

LOT 148
Ave. 3, Old 51
Owner - Henry Buff
Bernard Fauth - Mar. 15, 1839, age 42 yrs.
Mrs. Dorotha Fauth - Jan. 5, 1871, age 77 yrs.
Lucy A. Fauth - Mar. 8, 1848, age 26 yrs.
Lt. B. Fauth - Grimes Bat. CSA.
Henry Buff - June 20, 1863, age 63 yrs.
Eva C. Buff - Mar. 15, 1859, age 53 yrs.
Winifred Durr - July 20, 1871, age 2 yrs.
F. Durr - Dec. 1, 1887, age 49 yrs.
Ann Amelia Fauth - Mar. 4, 1856, age 2 yrs.
Barbari Buff - Feb. 15, 1884, age 77 yrs.
Samuel Cutherell - 1833-1875, age 42 yrs.
Amelia V. Cutherell - 1838-1900, age 62 yrs.
Edward Buff - June 19, 1847, age 14 yrs.
Lucy Amelia Fauth - Oct. 6, 1850, age 3 yrs.

LOT 149
Ave. 2, Old 37
Owner - Robert Dickson

Jane Dickson - July 16, 1851, age 1 mo.
Mrs. Jane Dickson - Mar. 12, 1843, age 62 yrs.
Robert Dickson - Dec. 20, 1866, age 55 yrs.
James Henry Bogart - Oct. 20, 1866, age 47 yrs.
William S. Bogart - Sept. 22, 1892, age 72 yrs.
Florence G. Bogart - Dec. 14, 1926, age 85 yrs.
Dr. Marmaduke Francis Daughtry - Apr. 5, 1897, age 79 yrs.
Elizabeth Moody Daughtry - buried July 25, 1903, age 64 yrs.
Fanny Daughtry - July 11, 1868, age 52 yrs.

LOT 150
Ave. 3, Old 50
Owner - Samuel Brewer
John M. Herbert - June 8, 1812, age 33 yrs.
Alice V. Brewer - Aug. 25, 1855, age 6 yrs.
Samuel Brewer - Aug. 31, 1855, age 39 yrs.
Priscilla A. Brewer - Aug. 18, 1851, age 2 yrs.
Samuel T. Brewer - Nov. 11, 1844, age 3 mos.
Samuel Moore - Aug. 15, 1811, age 5 yrs.
Elizabeth Moore - wife of Samuel Moore.
Samuel Moore - May 28, 1850, age 50 yrs.
Virginia C. Selwyn - Nov. 5, 1813, age 15 yrs.
Eliza Carroll - buried Oct. 6, 1894, age 90 yrs.

LOT 151
Ave. 2, Old 36
Owner - William R. Guy
Susan J. Guy - Oct. 8, 1892, age 40 yrs.
William A. Guy - Sept. 3, 1927, age 76 yrs.
Mary E. Lawrence - Dec. 2, 1919, age 71 yrs.
Richard H. Williams - Nov. 20, 1904, age 52 yrs.
Guy M. Binderwald - May 26, 1901, age 10 mos.
Noah Adams - Dec. 23, 1903, age 73 yrs.
W. L. Guy - stillborn, May 22, 1902.
Margaret Daughtry - Sept. 23, 1892, age 37 yrs.
A. C. Adams - Dec. 5, 1901, age 80 yrs.
1 grave - no name.

LOT 152
Ave. 3, Old 149
Owner - S. B. Laylor or Taylor
William H. Laylor - 1852-1853.
Eleanor A. Laylor - 1855-1856.
Emma M. Powers - buried July 31, 1892, age 52 yrs.
Randel C. Revell, Sr. - 1813-1849.

Virginia C. Revell - 1814-1865.
William J. Revell - 1839-1864.
John T. Revell - 1847-1869.
George A. Revell - July 31, 1892, age 52 yrs., CSA.
Infant of G. A. and Martha Revell.

LOT 153
Ave. 2, Old 35
Owner - G. S. Ferguson
Robert H. Peed - buried Oct. 22, 1886, age 44 yrs.
Elizabeth S. Ferguson - buried Apr. 1, 1890, age 74 yrs.
John L. Ferguson - buried Jan. 4, 1892, age 36 yrs.
3 graves - no names.

LOT 154
Ave. 3
Owner - Sneed, N/H
Hellen Frances Richardson - Jan. 23, 1897, age 3 mos.
Richardson - stillborn of W. J. Richardson, July 9, 1905.
Myers - stillborn of C. H. and E. R. Myers, Mar. 28, 1809.
Rountree - stillborn, Apr. 14, 1899.
Virginia A. Griffin - buried Oct. 12, 1889, age 54 yrs.
4 graves - no names.

LOT 155
Ave. 2, Old 34
Owners - Myers and Williams
Welzey James Presnell - Nov. 12, 1968 (vault).
Mary E. Williams - Feb. 15, 1908, age 88 yrs.
Claymurt Williams - Apr. 29, 1919, age 68 yrs.
Sarah E. Williams - May 26, 1922, age 58 yrs.
Addie C. Cook - June 25, 1903, age 19 yrs.
J. H. Stearn - stillborn, buried Aug. 8, 1919.
John H. Stearn - May 25, 1936, age 48 yrs. 9 mos.

LOT 156
Ave. 3, Old 48
Owner - Madison Jordan
William Turpin Kilby - Oct. 1, 1895, age 67 yrs., CSA.
Lucrece Selah Kilby - Oct. 3, 1917, age 78 yrs.
Madison Jordan - Dec. 13, 1857, age 54 yrs.
Ann Eliza Jordan - May 30, 1892, age 76 yrs.
Josephus Wilson Jordan - died Jan. 10, 1865, age 21 yrs. Co. K,
    9th Va. Inf. CSA.
Sarah Wilson - May 20, 1862, age 81 yrs.

LOT 157
Ave. 2, Old 33
Owner - Esleeck, N/H
Ethel V. Foiles - buried Mar. 26, 1893, age 1 yr. 6 mos.
Mattie M. Esleeck - buried May 20, 1889, age 9 mos.
Maria M. Joiner - buried Apr. 19, 1886, age 8 mos.
George Henry Johnson - Sept. 18, 1908, age 78 yrs.
Clarke Joiner - buried Jan. 25, 1891, age 7 1/2 mos.
Emmett L. Whitehead - buried Feb. 12, 1894, age 7 yrs. 9 mos.
Thurman R. Whitehead - May 7, 1906, age 9 yrs.
George W. Joyner - buried Dec. 6, 1888, age 2 mos.
Hiram Foiles - May 5, 1900, age 6 mos.
Grace Whitehead - buried June 17, 1885, age 6 days.
Frank Hope Dashiell - Sept. 7, 1887, age 1 yr.
Harry Maywood Joiner - 1885-1886.
Hortense Omeca and Laura Green - infants of Isaac and Ann W.
   Esleeck.

LOT 158
Ave. 3, Old 47
Owner - R. G. Jones
6 graves - no names.
Robert Gaskins Jones - 1800-1879.
Agnes Nash Jones - 1806-1881.
Virginia L. Jones - Oct. 30, 1917, age 83 yrs.
Nellie Roche - 1866-1867.
Ida B. Sadler - buried May 18, 1884, age 2 yrs.
Mary E. Guathney - buried Apr. 6, 1888, age 10 days.
Walter J. Trafton - buried Aug. 25, 1889, age 68 yrs.

LOT 159
Ave. 2, Old 33
Owner - Albert E. West, S/H
Clyde E. West - Dec. 20, 1943, age 65 yrs.
Nell Watts West - June 22, 1963.
Albert Edward West - July 26, 1930, age 80 yrs.
Frances P. West - Feb. 13, 1933, age 79 yrs.
Lydia Ann Johnson - Jan. 1, 1901, age 69 yrs. 9 mos.
Mary Rebecca Miller - buried June 1, 1894, age 15 yrs. 7 mos.
Grace Whitehead - buried June 17, 1885, age 6 days.

LOT 160
Ave. 3, Old 46
Owner - Philip Fauth
Elsie Bishop - Oct. 5, 1957, age 67 yrs.

Laura Jane Bishop - Dec. 8, 1943, age 83 yrs.
Mr. Bishop - Sept. 1884, age 65 yrs.
John Bishop - buried Aug. 29, 1893, age 2 days.
Charles H. Bishop - May 2, 1933, age 78 yrs.
William A. Bishop - Mar. 19, 1852, age 12 yrs.
Philip J. Fauth - Feb. 18, 1860, age 2 yrs.
Ella R. Dowdy - buried June 6, 1891, age 3 1/2 yrs.
Maude Bishop - buried June 16, 1891, age 1 1/2 yrs.
David Bain - Aug. 2, 1883, age 32 yrs.

LOT 161
Ave. 2, Old 32
Owner - W. H. Parks
Elizabeth Choates - buried Oct. 20, 1883, age 25 yrs.
William Henry Harrison Parks - July 27, 1836, age 9 mos. 1 day.
Mary Choate Bilisoly - Feb. 5, 1916, 63 yrs.
Bartholomew C. Bilisoly - Nov. 20, 1931, age 60 yrs.
Lucile C. Bilisoly - Apr. 15, 1952, age 68 yrs.
Eugene A. Bilisoly - Apr. 13, 1936, age 60 yrs.
Paul C. Bilisoly - Dec. 1, 1944, age 66 yrs.

LOT 162
Ave. 3, Old 45
Owner - C. S. Myers
Mary Elizabeth Myers - June 13, 1843, age 10 yrs.
Ardilsey Myers - May 26, 1853, age 51 yrs.
Charles S. Myers - Aug. 25, 1855, age 59 yrs.
Ellen F. Myers - Sept. 8, 1855, age 28 yrs.
Maria Jane Myers - July 23, 1915, age 83 yrs.
Robert W. Myers - 9th Va. Inf. CSA.
Charles T. Myers - Mar. 7, 1908, age 54 yrs.
Charles N. Myers - Aug. 29, 1855, age 8 yrs.
Lewis Myers - Sept. 17, 1836, age 3 yrs. 10 mos.
Infant of C. H. and E. Myers - Apr. 11, 1908, age 9 days.

LOT 163
Ave. 2, Old 31
Owner - Margaret Armistead
John Collins Armistead - May 29, 1915, age 39 yrs.
Francis N. Armistead - buried Nov. 11, 1892, age 21 yrs.
Mrs. Sarah Miller - buried July 5, 1885, age 55 yrs.
Louise Armistead - Mar. 8, 1953, age 74 yrs.
John C. Armistead - Nov. 29, 1915.
Laura Collins Armistead - Aug. 31, 1895, age 58 yrs.

Beverly Arthur Armistead - Nov. 26, 1886, age 52 yrs., C 1, 18th
   Va. Calv. CSA.
F. Noble Armistead - Nov. 10, 1892, age 21 yrs.
Eunice Bayton - 1847, age 65 yrs. (Jan. 7, 1847).
Capt. Beverly Bayton - 1834 (June 20, 1834, age 60 yrs.).
Ann Eliza Bayton - 1900 (Aug. 14, 1900).
Catherine Armistead - 1891.
Lt. F. N. Armistead - died Apr. 14, 1841, age 35 yrs., USMC.
Catherine Harris - 1841, infant.
E. Armistead - (boy).
Lt. F. N. Armistead - died July 3, 1861, age 27 yrs., son of F. N.
   and Catherine L. Armistead, CSA.

LOT 164
Ave. 3, Old 44
Owners - Gayle, S/H - Tonkin, N/H
8 graves - no names.
Sarah F. Gayle - buried Oct. 22, 1886, age 80 yrs.
Seamon Gayle - buried Nov. 25, 1886, age 82 yrs.
William F. Tonkin - buried Jan. 8, 1892, age 29 yrs.
Adj. Leaven Gayle - died Feb. 2, 1901, age 62 yrs., 12th Ala. Inf.
   CSA.
Col. B. B. Gayle - 12th Ala. Inf. CSA.
Capt. W. F. Tonkins - 9th Va. Inf. CSA.
Cornelius Beazley, buried Sept. 2, 1886, age 59 yrs.
Sarah Gayle - Jan. 7, 1887, age 39 yrs.
Mary F. Tonkin - buried Aug. 3, 1892, age 54 yrs.
W. F. Tonkin - Sept. 13, 1912, age 77 yrs.

LOT 165
Ave. 2, Old 30
Owner - Enoch Choate
Miss R. A. Turner - buried Apr. 4, 1884, age 80 yrs.
Mrs. Sarah Camm - Mar. 2, 1846, age 79 yrs.
Henrietta K. Choate - May 24, 1908, age 44 yrs.
Thomas V. Willoughby - Feb. 3, 1835, age 26 yrs.
Margaret Tabb
Florence and Jervey Choate - children of James C. and Eliza J.
   Choate.
Mrs. Margaret Choate - Mar. 6, 1837, age 51 yrs.
Capt. Enoch Choate - Sept. 27, 1833, age 47 yrs.

LOT 166
Ave. 3, Old 43
Owner - Arthur Emmerson

Mary Emmerson - Nov. 5, 1937, age 77 yrs.
Louise Emmerson - May 24, 1907, age 87 yrs.
Arthur Emmerson - Aug. 7, 1918, age 49 yrs.
John Emmerson - Mar. 12, 1885, age 63 yrs., CSA.
Susan Barron Cocke Emmerson - Dec. 25, 1926, age 86 yrs.
Arthur Emmerson - Dec. 15, 1870.
Annie Emmerson - May 21, 1953, age 91 yrs.
Mary A. Emmerson - Sept. 6, 1859.
Charles E. Wilkins - buried Nov. 13, 1886, age 5 yrs.

LOT 167
Ave. 2, Old 29
Owner - John Collins
9 graves - no names.
Peter Heron - 1778-1839, age 60 yrs.
Sophia A. W. Collins - Jan. 3, 1850, age 26 yrs.
A. E. Collins - 9th Va. Inf. CSA.
W. B. Collins - 9th Va. Inf. CSA.
John A. Stanwood - buried Sept. 15, 1886, age 31 yrs.
Sykes - stillborn, buried Jan. 3, 1896.

LOT 168
Ave. 4, Old 7
Owner - W. O. Hope
Robert E. Lee Wood - 1866-1923, age 56 yrs.
John Powell Wood - 1878-1923, age 46 yrs.
Virginia Sparrow - June 20, 1952, age 64 yrs.
Hugh Stanley Hope - Feb. 11, 1958, age 60 yrs.
William M. Hope - July 29, 1937, age 46 yrs.
Katie Deans Hope - July 18, 1900, age 17 yrs.
William Owens Hope - June 10, 1924, age 71 yrs.
Katie Virginia Hope - Dec. 1, 1930, age 73 yrs.

LOT 169
Ave. 3, Old 6
Owner - William A. West
Bettie F. West - 1841-1908, age 67 yrs.
William A. West - 1841-1907, age 66 yrs., Sgt. 61st Va. Inf. CSA.
Anna Wilson - stillborn, Aug. 9, 1932.
Monument

LOT 170
Ave. 3, Old 8
Owner - William G. Maupin
Samuel D. Maupin - Oct. 8, 1950, age 95 yrs.

Alliene Maupin - Dec. 16, 1949, age 91 yrs.
George Maupin - Jan. 3, 1942, age 80 yrs.
Florence Brayley Maupin - Dec. 1977, age 85 yrs.
Ruth Maupin - Feb. 17, 1938, age 78 yrs.
Dr. Edward Griffith Maupin - May 18, 1937, age 86 yrs.
Matilda Dawson Maupin - Jan. 11, 1927, age 74 yrs.
William Gabriel Maupin, Jr. - Jan. 31, 1926, age 78 yrs.

LOT 170
Ave. 4, Old 5
Owner - William G. Maupin
James Foley Maupin - Aug. 23, 1915.
Edmoria Tomlin Maupin - July 11, 1923, age 65 yrs.
W. M. Maupin - Feb. 13, 1951, age 61 yrs.
Maupin - stillborn, Jan. 26, 1929.
Infant of James Maupin - buried Mar. 3, 1892, age 5 hrs.
Mary Maupin - Apr. 6, 1874.
William Gabriel Maupin - Jan. 10, 1892, age 71 yrs.
Ann Foley Maupin - Apr. 12, 1908, age 83 yrs.
Nannie Maria Maupin - May 18, 1922, age 76 yrs.

LOT 171
Ave. 3, Old 9
Owner - John W. Wood
Charles McA. Wood - Jan. 29, 1899, age 27 yrs.
Ethel Stores Wood Lilly - died Sept. 22, 1922, age 35 yrs.
Elizabeth F. Choat - Mar. 9, 1929, age 79 yrs.
Edna Roane - buried July 9, 1891, age 1 mo.
Rosannah H. Godfrey - Aug. 9, 1896, age 68 yrs.
John J. Godfrey - Jan. 12, 1914, age 63 yrs.
Rebecca J. Wood - Apr. 18, 1925, age 70 yrs.
John W. Wood - Feb. 11, 1911, age 69 yrs., CSA.
Silas Draper - June 20, 1887, age 64 yrs.
Frances Jane Draper - June 15, 1904, age 78 yrs.

LOT 172
Ave. 4, Old 4
Owner - D. K. Snyder
Kate Eva Snyder - Nov. 26, 1911, age 56 yrs.
Mariah K. Snyder - Jan. 6, 1919, age 48 yrs.
Daniel K. Snyder - Nov. 25, 1938, age 85 yrs.
Katherine D. Snyder - 1877-1905, age 27 yrs.
Annie May Snyder - Nov. 22, 1887, age 3 yrs.
Leisle McM. Snyder - July 6, 1972 (vault).
Snyder - stillborn of M. C. Snyder, buried Apr. 22, 1908.

Snyder - stillborn of M. C. Snyder, buried Aug. 20, 1909.
Stillborn - buried Aug. 16, 1918.
Samuel W. Armistead - Feb. 2, 1895, age 33 yrs.
Rosa Edna Dewberry - Jan. 18, 1910, age 34 yrs.
Clarence Snyder - Apr. 8, 1905, age 27 yrs. 10 mos.
Rose Edna Snyder - Sept. 20, 1929, age 1 yr. 9 mos.
Daughtery - stillborn of Rev. J. D. Daughtery, Apr. 28, 1891.

LOT 173
Ave. 3, Old 10
Owner - W. E. Hurst
Ann Cordelia Hurst - Dec. 1, 1920, age 88 yrs.
Lewis R. Poessel - Nov. 24, 1910, age 49 yrs., Chief Yoeman USN.
Robert E. Hurst - May 10, 1887, age 1 yr.
William B. Hurst - Mar. 11, 1887.
Robert L. Hurst - Feb. 27, 1916, age 64 yrs.
William Edward Hurst - July 27, 1933, age 74 yrs.

LOT 174
Ave. 4, Old 3
Owner - Fanny E. Burns
Joseph F. Williams - Aug. 14, 1965.
Blanche B. Williams
James Mulligan Burns - Aug. 16, 1966 (vault).
Emery Burns - May 9, 1885, age 55 yrs.
Fanny Elizabeth Burns - Aug. 29, 1887, age 45 yrs.
Blanche Estelle Burns - Aug. 10, 1893, age 20 yrs.
Claude C. Burns - July 8, 1940, age 72 yrs.
Meary A. Burns - Dec. 1, 1928, age 60 yrs.
Claude E. Burns - Oct. 14, 1964.

LOT 175
Ave. 3, Old 11
Owner - Mary Beaton Stevens
Julia Leigh Gibbs - June 28, 1900, age 3 yrs.
Martha Leigh Gibbs - Jan. 2, 1972 (vault).
William Robins Stevens - Apr. 13, 1943, age 75 yrs.
Mary Francis Beaton Stevens - Mar. 21, 1912, age 83 yrs.
R. B. Stevens - Nov. 19, 1889, age 74 yrs.
J. K. B. Stevens - Apr. 28, 1880, age 17 yrs.
Nannie Lilly Stevens Mills - Mar. 18, 1927, age 65 yrs.
J. H. Mills - July 19, 1905, age 54 yrs.
Mary Beaton Gibbs - Oct. 12, 1979 (vault).
Matthew Lee Gibbs - Sept. 1, 1947, age 86 yrs.

Mary S. Gibbs - Jan. 9, 1947, age 81 yrs.
Sophronie R. Stevens - Jan. 30, 1898, age 72 yrs.

LOT 176
Ave. 4, Old 2
Owner - Virginia Plummer
Laban Jackson Plummer - June 6, 1919, age 61 yrs.
Lovie Ann Plummer - July 29, 1937, age 70 yrs.
Virginia C. Plummer - Oct. 23, 1900, age 70 yrs.
Adelaide Plummer Cherry - Apr. 22, 1939, age 81 yrs.
Alonza Lockwood Cherry - Dec. 8, 1918, age 40 yrs.
Daniel W. Plummer - Dec. 24, 1907, age 58 yrs.
Willis H. Plummer - Nov. 16, 1876, age 22 yrs.
Willis Plummer - Dec. 29, 1860, age 46 yrs.
Mary E. Tucker - Nov. 6, 1884, age 21 yrs., removed from Cedar
Grove to Deep Creek.
William Plummer, Sr. - buried Jan. 8, 1885.
William Plummer, Jr. - buried Jan. 8, 1885.

LOT 177
Ave. 3, Old 12
Owner - David E. Williams
David Williams - 1808-1895, age 86 yrs., CSA.
Thirza Williams - 1809-1889, age 79 yrs.
Grace Maupin Williams - Apr. 11, 1955, age 76 yrs.
Luther J. Williams - 1831-1900, age 69 yrs., CSA.
Harriett N. Williams - 1839-1917, age 78 yrs.
Hattie Lee Williams - 1881-1940, age 58 yrs.
Charles E. Williams - 1867-1935, age 67 yrs.
Ruby R. Williams - 1887-1935, age 48 yrs.
Alice Rebecca Williams - 1846-1931, age 84 yrs.
David E. Williams - 1844-1903, age 55 yrs., CSA.

LOT 178
Ave. 4, Old 1
Owner - Richard T. Barnes
Laura King Barnes - Apr. 16, 1933, age 66 yrs.
Richard T. Barnes - Apr. 17, 1912, age 69 yrs.
Golis A. Barnes - 1876-1912, age 35 yrs.
Herman H. Burmester - Dec. 30, 1961, age 86 yrs.
Bessie Burmester - Apr. 18, 1950, age 61 yrs.
Sallie Lee Barnes - buried Feb. 20, 1889, age 2 yrs.
Annie Sue Barnes - buried Aug. 19, 1892, age 2 yrs. 18 days.
Richard T. Barnes - buried Aug. 8, 1892, age 2 yrs. 7 days.

LOT 179
Ave. 3, Old JP1
Owner - Confederate States Army
William Delanzanne - Jan. 23, 1887, age 63 yrs., CSA.
John Hargrove - buried Feb. 2, 1890, age 53 yrs., CSA.
Charles C. Small - Mar. 18, 1907, age 63 yrs., CSA.
Osmond Peters - June 30, 1927, age 83 yrs., 2nd Co. Independent Signal Corp. CSA.

LOT 179
Ave. 3, Old JP1
Owner - Confederate States Army
I. M. Levitte - Co. B, 12th Va. Inf. CSA.
J. W. Griffin - Pvt. Portsmouth, Lt. Artillery Co., CSA.
A. A. Coleman - Nov. 22, 1885, age 40 yrs., CSA.
John Richard Laurence - July 4, 1903, age 65 yrs., CSA.
Joseph H. Barrett - age 81 yrs., CSA.
Wilson W. Holstead - Pvt. Co. A, 3rd Va. Inf. CSA.
A. Spivey - Pvt. Co. D, 54th N.C. Inf. CSA.
R. H. Herring - Pvt. Co. 1, 9th Va. Inf. CSA.
McKenny Lewis - Sgt. Co. 1, 9th Va. Inf. CSA.
Yound Humphries - Pvt. Co. D, 61st Va. Inf. CSA.
J. E. Smith - Co. C, 6th Va. Inf. CSA.
James T. Weston - Naval Batt. CSA.
W. J. Smith - 6th Va. Inf. CSA.
James A. Walker - CSA.
Augustine M. Hope - Mar. 2, 1909, age 67 yrs., CSA.

LOT 180
Ave. 4, Old 0
Owner - John Murdaugh
Fannie Murdaugh Downing - daughter of J. W. and M. W. Murdaugh, May 6, 1894, age 62 yrs.
Charles Downing - Dec. 16, 1892, age 40 yrs.
John W. Murdaugh - Nov. 21, 1842.
Margaret Walen Murdaugh - wife of John W. Murdaugh, Apr. 11, 1839.
John W. Murdaugh, Jr. - Sept. 1, 1867, Lt. CSN.
Margaret A. Murdaugh - wife of William H. Wilson, June 7, 1874.
Nannie C. Murdaugh - May 5, 1903, age 68 yrs.
William H. Murdaugh - Died Dec 28, 1801, age 75 yrs., USN and CSN Capt.

LOT 181
Ave. 3, Old 200
Owner - William G. Wheeler
William Easly - 1850-1922, age 72 yrs.
M. Louisa Easly - 1855-1928, age 72 yrs.
Susan Imogene Wheeler - 1876.
William S. Wheeler - May 31, 1859.
Maria Louisa Wheeler - Nov. 6, 1898, age 71 yrs.
William C. Wheeler - Aug. 15, 1900, age 71 yrs.
Eliza H. Wheeler - July 8, 1888, age 88 yrs.
Dulton Wheeler - June 12, 1870, age 49 yrs.

LOT 182
Ave. 4, Old 177
Owner - Dr. Joseph Schoolfield
Lt. Robert D. Page - died Nov. 13, 1815, age 29 yrs., US Marine
    Corp.
Mary Imogene Page - Jan. 1, 1847, age 29 yrs.
Joseph N. Schoolfield, M.D. - July 19, 1871, age 59.
Mary Slade Schoolfield - Aug. 18, 1865, age 46 yrs.
Mary Josephine Schoolfield - July 10, 1813, age 10 mos.
Joseph Schoolfield - 1851-1862, age 10 yrs.
Mary Ann Schoolfield - Nov. 30, 1862, age 71 yrs.
Dr. Joseph Schoolfield - Sept. 26, 1850, age 66 yrs.
Benjamin Barroud Schoolfield - Jan. 13, 1850, age 32 yrs.

LOT 183
Ave. 3, Old 199
Owners - Clark and Tyler, N/H
Julia H. Tyler - July 16, 1910, age 69 yrs.
Allcamp - stillborn, Jan. 14, 1901.
Mary W. Tyler - Nov. 16, 1818, age 32 yrs.
Capt. Henry Tyler - buried Oct. 24, 1869, age 63 yrs. (CSA ?).

LOT 184
Ave. 4, Old 176
Owner - M. M. Anderson
Ann Louise Potts - May 30, 1858, age 39 yrs.
Louisa Gordon Anderson - 1789-1867.
Eliza Rudd Anderson - Nov. 10, 1867, age 50 yrs.
Joseph S. Anderson - Apr. 15, 1871, age 23 yrs.
Thomas, Anna, Michael, and Winfred - children of M. M. and
    Eliza Anderson.
M. M. Anderson - Sept. 29, 1894, age 73 yrs.
Mrs. Marion A. King - Aug. 3, 1935, age 90 yrs.

LOT 185
Old 199
Owners - Clark and Tyler, S/H
Frank H. Fletcher - buried Sept. 14, 1886, age 19 days.
Bettie Fletcher - age 1 day.

LOT 186
Ave. 4, Old 175
Owner - John Tart, N/H
John Tart - 1802-1885, age 82 yrs.
Barbara A. Tart - 1805-1878, age 72 yrs.
John V. Tart - 1832-1872, age 39 yrs.
Mary F. Godwin - Aug. 6, 1909, age 71 yrs.
Charles W. Godwin - died Jan. 24, 1907, age 74 yrs., 17th Va.
   Inf. CSA.
John L. Matthews - Aug. 19, 1902, age 22 yrs. 11 mos.
Susie Ellis Matthews - Apr. 7, 1885, age 24 yrs.

LOT 187
Ave. 3, Old 198
Owner - Anderton
Isaac N. Anderton - Nov. 18, 1906, age 50 yrs.
Alice L. Anderton - Nov. 24, 1922, age 18 yrs.
Jennie Hope Anderton - Dec. 4, 1887, age 2 yrs. 5 mos.
William T. Anderton - died Apr. 15, 1913, age 74 yrs., Co. G, 9th
   Va. Inf. CSA.
Ann A. Anderton - Dec. 23, 1913, age 75 yrs.
Sadie A. Anderton - May 9, 1904, age 20 yrs.
Henry Heemann Gunnery - died July 24, 1940, age 60 yrs. 10
   mos., Sgt. Marine Corp. and USN.
Lucille S. Heemann - Oct. 9, 1945, age 68 yrs.
Cora Lee Laurence - Sept. 5, 1934, age 72 yrs.
William Henry Laurence - Nov. 1, 1931, age 77 yrs.
Sarah J. Dewberry - Aug. 20, 1928, age 64 yrs.
William J. Anderton - Feb. 11, 1908, age 47 yrs.
Florence V. Laurence - Dec. 4, 1894.
Willie T. A. Laurence - Dec. 14, 1893.
Bessie L. Laurence - Aug. 4, 1888.
Gracie C. Laurence - Apr. 2, 1886.

LOT 188
Ave. 4, Old 175
Owner - C. C. Virnelson, S/H
Margaret V. Virnelson - Mar. 23, 1919, age 65 yrs.
Columbus C. Virnelson - Feb. 26, 1918, age 68 yrs.

Williard Humplett - Nov. 6, 1966, age 56 yrs., cremation.
John James Humphlett - Dec. 14, 1949.
Maggie May Humphlett - Oct. 4, 1973.
John Howell - Oct. 29, 1900, 9th Va. Inf. CSA.
John James Humphlett - above was moved from Oak Grove to
   Cedar Grove, Sept. 30, 1953.

LOT 188
Ave. 4, Old 175
Owner - C. C. Virnelson, S/H
Estelle H. Virnelson - Oct. 20, 1890, age 1 yr.
Martha J. Jamerson - Dec. 28, 1893, age 67 yrs.
Anna B. Virnelson - May 19, 1921, age 46 yrs.

LOT 189
Ave. 3, Old 197
Owner - W. D. Wood
Elizabeth Ann Butt - June 5, 1907, age 80 yrs.
H. Clay Wood - Apr. 9, 1900, age 54 yrs.
George W. Butt - Dec. 17, 1853, age 34 yrs.
Sarah R. Wood - Apr. 14, 1886, age 81 yrs.
William D. Wood - Mar. 29, 1859, age 64 yrs., War 1812.
Augustus H. Wood - Sept. 30, 1865, age 16 yrs.
Walter M. Murfree - stillborn, May 22, 1891.
Murfree infant - daughter, July 9, 1891, age 1 mo.
Benjamin F. Wood - Oct. 3, 1860, age 24 yrs.
Sadie J. Tee - Apr. 12, 1870, age 20 yrs.
Sadie Wood Tee - 1870, age 4 mos.
Eva Wood Murfree - May 29, 1891, age 30 yrs.
W. J. Wood - buried Sept. 5, 1887, age 52 yrs., 4th Va. Bat. CSA.

LOT 190
Ave. 4, Old 174
Owner - John O. Moore, N/H
Thomas Herbert Edwards - Jan. 1, 1903, age 1 yr.
O. R. Moore - June 24, 1895, age 7 mos.
Charles P. Orr - Jan. 5, 1898, age 9 yrs. 2 mos.
A. E. Moore - (my mother), Dec. 28, 1846.
Mary E. Edwards - Oct. 15, 1916, age 78 yrs.
Capt. H. E. Orr - Mar. 29, 1892, age 62 yrs., 61st Va. Inf. CSA.
Annie S. Edwards - May 31, 1903, age 35 yrs.
John A. Edwards - died June 8, 1939, age 74 yrs., Boilermaker
   USN Spanish American War.
Amos W. Edwards - buried Apr. 23, 1891, age 59 yrs., 9th Va.
   Inf. CSA.

LOT 191
Ave. 3, Old M
Owner - D. Fritts, N/H
David Fritts - Jan. 9, 1856, age 21 yrs. 10 mos.

LOT 192
Ave. 4, Old 174
Owner - Nicholas Shacklock, S/H
Nicholas Shacklock - May 3, 1892, age 70 yrs.
Daniel W. Shacklock - Oct. 8, 1899, age 48 yrs.
William H. Shacklock - Aug. 9, 1905, age 29 yrs.
Lulie H. Shacklock - Aug. 30, 1889, age 36 yrs.
Augustus Shacklock - Aug. 4, 1900, age 27 yrs.
Martha B. Knapp - July 21, 1890, age 85 yrs.

LOT 193
Ave. 3, Old M
Owner - Holden, S/H
Margaret Oinas - July 9, 1847, age 36 yrs.

LOT 194
Ave. 4, Old 173
Owners - Hardwick and Knapp
Glady Simmons Hardy and Tudor Frith Hardy
Catherine Kearns - May 16, 1847, age 23 yrs.
John N. Knapp - 1797-1881.
Martha B. Knapp - 1890 (See Lot 192).
Catherine M. Horton Hardwick - Dec. 20, 1857, age 26 yrs.
Lt. Frederick J. Simmons - Oct. 14, 1890, age 54 yrs., USRCS.
Emma Virginia Simmons - Apr. 9, 1927, age 82 yrs.
Infant Sarah, Martha, Josephine Simmons.
Catherine Allen Russell - Mar. 19, 1888, age 3 mos. 9 days.
Mary A. Cuthrell - May 4, 1884, age 31 yrs.
Hacinda C. Russell - Dec. 3, 1888, age 31 yrs.
Ernest H. Simmons - Feb. 21, 1888, age 5 mos.

LOT 195
Ave. 3, Old 195
Owner - John E. Jarvis, N/H
John E. Jarvis - Nov. 27, 1884, age 62 yrs.
Sallie Jarvis - Sept. 3, 1881.
Elizabeth C. Jarvis - Feb. 4, 1897, age 74 yrs.
Miss Bessie Jarvis - Jan. 18, 1888, age 39 yrs.
Lucy H. Jarvis - Jan. 26, 1885, age 77 yrs.
Virginia E. Rogers - Jan. 18, 1895, age 64 yrs.

LOT 196
Ave. 4, Old 172
Owner - I. N. McAlpine
Samuel B. Browne - 1798-1848, age 49 yrs.
Yates N. Browne - 1800-1891, age 91 yrs.
Gabriella G. Browne - 1836-1849, age 13 yrs.
Charles Robert McAlpine - Feb. 13, 1876, age 59 yrs., Maj. 61st
Va. Inf. CSA.
Elizabeth Cason McAlpine - Sept. 24, 1898, age 69 yrs.
Yates McAlpine Wilson - Sept. 26, 1923, age 70 yrs.
Charles, Robert, Elizabeth, Virginia B., Annie M., and Charline
R. - infant children of Charles Robert and Elizabeth Cason
McAlpine.
William Lewis McAlpine - July 28, 1911, age 52 yrs.
James F. McAlpine - June 19, 1897, age 26 yrs.
Anne and Frederick A. McAlpine - infant children of C. R. and
E. C. McAlpine.
Anne Lewis Cason - 1804-1872, age 67 yrs.

LOT 197
Ave. 3, Old 195
Owner - William Pleasant, S/H
Josiah Pleasant - Mar. 15, 1857, age 83 yrs.

LOT 198
Ave. 4, Old 171
Owners - Haynes and Brounley
Charles Cleaves - Jan. 28, 1861, age 2 yrs. 9 mos.
Capt. L. T. Cleaves - 9th Va. Inf. CSA.
Susan Daughtrey Eason - 1847-1920, age 72 yrs.
Mary A. Cross - 1845-1930, age 84 yrs.
James A. Cross - 1821-1890, age 67 yrs.
Rebecca Daughtry - Dec. 1, 1889, age 63 yrs.
John Brounley - no date.
Mary A. Brounley - no date.
Walter Brounley - Jan. 17, 1886, age 6 yrs.

LOT 199
Ave. 3, Old 194
Owners - J. D. Griffin and W. W. Martin, N/H
Martha S. Grant - Aug. 5, 1928, age 79 yrs.
Mary Lillian Griffin - 1882-1937, age 54 yrs.
Lt. Joel D. Griffin - Mar. 8, 1937, age 80 yrs., USN.

Lena Grant Martin - Jan. 27, 1926, age 48 yrs.
William W. Martin - July 3, 1943, age 77 yrs.
Emma Martin - June 7, 1941, age 68 yrs.

LOT 200
Ave. 3, Old 194
Owner - W. D. Fitchett, S/H
Mary P. White - Nov. 19, 1901, age 81 yrs.
Eva Fitchett - July 18, 1959, age 88 yrs.
William A. C. Fitchett - April 12, 1949, age 76 yrs.
Marietta E. Fitchett - Apr. 19, 1916, age 64 yrs.
W. Dines Fitchett - Oct. 23, 1944, age 70 yrs.
Kenneth W. Fitchett - Aug. 15, 1902, age 27 yrs.

LOT 201
Ave. 3, Old 193
Owner - J. W. Cooper, N/H
Katie C. Smith - Apr. 5, 1972.
Claudius F. Smith - Mar. 12, 1963.
W. J. Cooper - Feb. 22, 1945, age 56 yrs.
Laura F. Cooper - Dec. 9, 1927, age 60 yrs.
John W. Cooper - Aug. 3, 1932, age 66 yrs.

LOT 202
Ave. 4, Old 170
Owner - L. W. Howland
J. E. Anderson - stillborn, May 31, 1903.
Ann E. G. Holladay - Dec. 24, 1931, age 71 yrs.
M. J. Howland - 1836-1870, age 42 yrs.
James Gustavus Holladay Mitchell - Apr. 18, 1963.
Sally B. Holladay - May 2, 1948, age 74 yrs.
Florence V. Howland - 1846-1860, age 14 yrs.
William J. Howland - Jan. 22, 1854, age 52 yrs.
Dr. Gray Holladay - Nov. 26, 1942, age 72 yrs.
Mildred Holladay - Oct. 2, 1950, age 83 yrs.
Mary J. Howland - 1826-1970, age 44 yrs.

LOT 203
Ave. 3, Old 193
Owners - Wilder and Parson, S/H
Sgt. Robert L. Taylor - died July 30, 1908, age 38 yrs., Co. L,
    4th Va. Inf., Spanish American War.
George Washington Ferrell - Mar. 13, 1908, age 16 yrs.
Addie Louise Ferrell - June 16, 1917, age 5 days.
William Nelson Taylor - July 4, 1907, age 2 mos.

Marion Raymond Taylor - May 23, 1912, age 8 mos.
G. E. McPherson - Oct. 20, 1918, age 63 yrs.
George Nelson McPherson - Dec. 29, 1904, age 59 yrs.
Marion E. Taylor - Apr. 11, 1922, age 46 yrs.

LOT 204
Old 169
Owner - Pinner
William H. Peirce - Co. K, 9th Va. Inf. Va. Vol. CSA.
Capt. Hanze - his grave the Ocean (To the memory of).
Dorcas Millar - 1845.

LOT 205
Ave. 3, Old 192
Owner - I. McRea
John Wingfield McRea - died Sept. 30, 1855, age 27 yrs. (yellow fever).
Mary B. McRea - buried Jan. 24, 1891, age 58 yrs.

LOT 206
Ave. 4, Old N
Owner - W. H. Peters
Ester Peters - 1847-1852.
Richard Peters - 1857-1858.
Washington Peters, M.D. - 1849-1891, age 39 yrs.
William H. Peters - 1816-1901, age 86 yrs.
Mary A. Reed Peters - 1817-1904, age 87 yrs.
Frank Peters - 1853-1920, age 67 yrs.
William R. Peters - 1843-1913, age 70 yrs., Signal Corp. CSA.
Elizabeth M. Peters - 1820-1904, age 84 yrs.
Capt. Osmond Peters - Feb. 18, 1886, age 70 yrs., CSN.
Martha A. T. Peters - 1822-1855.
Martha C. Peters - 1793-1849.
James N. Peters - 1826-1844.
Frederic C. Peters - July 18, 1902, age 73 yrs.
Eugene W. Peters - July 4, 1885, age 2 yrs.

LOT 207
Ave. 3, Old 69
Owner - William Duffee
Fannie Duffee - buried Aug. 10, 1896, age 76 yrs.
Charles E. Duffee - May 25, 1920, age 74 yrs.
Mary Fletcher Duffee - Apr. 26, 1908, age 63 yrs.
L. Lee Duffee - Sept. 1896, age 1 yr. 7 mos.
Walter M. Duffee - died Apr. 26, 1908, Co. L, 2nd Va. Inf.,

Spanish American War.
William Duffee - Sept. 3, 1875, age 74 yrs.
Ann Duffee - Feb. 24, 1845, age 49 yrs.
W. D. Neville - buried Apr. 6, 1890, age 51 yrs., 9th Va. Inf. CSA.
Charles R. Duffee - June 23, 188-, age 15 yrs.
Charles Duffee - July 14, 1906, age 9 mos.

LOT 208
Ave. 4, Old 82
Owner - Richard W. Baugh
Lt. L. H. White - 3rd Va. Inf. CSA.
Richard W. Baugh - July 27, 1856, age 67 yrs.
Mary J. Baugh - June 22, 1877, age 86 yrs.
Richard W. Baugh - Aug. 19, 1839, age 1 day.
J. R. White - buried Mar. 6, 1897, age 70 yrs.
Imogene Love White - buried Feb. 2, 1894, age 26 yrs.
Child J. R. W. - buried Dec. 17, 1883.

LOT 209
Ave. 3, Old 68
Owners - Cushing and Neville
Willis C. Neville - 1866-1921, age 56 yrs.
Wendell Cushing - Oct. 24, 1840, age 34 yrs.
L. Virginia Long - June 18, 1856, age 27 yrs.
Mary E. C. Neville - 1835-1917, age 82 yrs.
Willis H. Neville - 1839-1882, age 43 yrs.
Mary A. Cushing - July 26, 1855, age 40 yrs. (yellow fever).
Frank L. Neville - Apr. 2, 1912, age 1 yr.

LOT 210
Old 81
Owner - Margaret Ann Myers, N/H
Victoria E. Griffin - Dec. 22, 1866, age 21 yrs.
Margaret Frances Myers - Aug. 3, 1838.
Margaret Ann Myers - Sept. 29, 1835.

LOT 211
Ave. 3, Old 67
Owners - Talbot and Bernard
Margaret J. Bernard - child of O. and M. J. Bernard.
Allen O. Bernard - child of O. and M. J. Bernard
Martha J. Bernard - Aug. 22, 1813, age 33 yrs.
O. Bernard - Aug. 5, 1866, age 68 yrs.
John Talbot - Sept. 1864, age 78 yrs.

Fanny Talbot - July 2, 1865.
Fanny Bernard Capps - Jan. 30, 1885, age 59 yrs.
Overton Bernard Capps - Dec. 21, 1875, age 19 yrs.
Alice M. Littleton - Oct. 18, 1892, age 54 yrs.
Lulie V. Littleton - Aug. 11, 1886, age 15 yrs. 6 mos.

LOT 212
Ave. 4, Old 81
Owner - Griffin Edwards, S/H
J. Griffin Edwards - Mar. 27, 1912, age 41 yrs.
William N. Walker - Sept. 24, 1966 (vault).
Martha N. Edwards - Jan. 1, 1953, age 82 yrs.
Little Carl - "God knows best"
Isabel Edwards - July 12, 1941, age 92 yrs.
Griffin Fauntleroy Edwards - died May 14, 1905, age 61 yrs.,
Adut. 61st Va. Inf. CSA.

LOT 213
Ave. 3, Old 66
Owner - William G. Webb
Sarah H. Pearce - Jan. 15, 1870.
Charlotte L. Webb - Nov. 30, 1885, age 74 yrs.
William G. Webb - Dec. 16, 1868.
J. Pearce - Constructor CSN.
Martha E. Webb - Apr. 15, 1857, age 12 yrs.

LOT 214
Ave. 4, Old 80
Owner - Henry V. Niemeyer
John C. Niemeyer - May 13, 1933, age 69 yrs.
May Wooten Niemeyer - June 25, 1909, age 43 yrs.
Virginia A. Niemeyer - Nov. 4, 1908, age 81 yrs.
Martha Caroline Niemeyer - 1825-1908, age 82 yrs.
Henry Victor Niemeyer - Aug. 22, 1883, age 74 yrs.
Charles F. Niemeyer - Sept. 21, 1834, age 33 yrs.
Henry Woodis Niemeyer - Apr. 7, 1862, age 29 yrs., CSN.
Susan Matilda Niemeyer - Aug. 21, 1875, age 45 yrs.
John N. Niemeyer - Feb. 13, 1951, age 49 yrs.

LOT 215
Old 66
Owner - Talbot G. Lester, S/H
Mary A. C. Lester - May 29, 1849, age 41 yrs.
Talbot G. Lester - June 25, 1841, age 36 yrs.
Sarah Ann Lester - July 14, 1849, age 10 yrs.

LOT 216
Ave. 4, Old 79
Owner - James M. Binford
John Rutter - June 20, 1845, age 77 yrs.
Sophia Rutter - Sept. 9, 1849, age 80 yrs.
Fannie B. Binford - June 1911, age 66 yrs.
Col. James M. Binford - Oct. 21, 1891, age 49 yrs., 23rd Va.
  Calv. CSA.
Mary Ann Binford - July 29, 1886, age 79 yrs.
James Marshall Binford - Dec. 28, 1851, age 53 yrs.
William Rutter - July 18, 1845, age 35 yrs.
Sophy L. Garlick - wife of John W. Garlick, M.D., died June 4,
  1856, age 30 yrs.
William Benford Garlick - Apr. 12, 1854, age 1 yr.
Carrie Gwathing Binford - Dec. 5, 1875.
James Marshall Binford - Dec. 20, 1874.
Octavia Knott Binford - Sept. 3, 1869.

LOT 217
Ave. 3, Old 65
Owners - James W. Cooke and Dr. T. Sanford Cooke
Mrs. Sarah Ann Watts - Sept. 6, 1893, age 85 yrs.
Mary E. A. Cooke - Mar. 5, 1889, age 64 yrs.
Capt. James Wallace Cooke - June 21, 1869, age 57 yrs.
Lechmere Cooke - Jan. 28, 1882, age 29 yrs.
Lara Simkins Cooke - Mar. 21, 1943.
W. H. Bayton - Sgt. died Nov. 8, 1866, age 27 yrs., served in CSA
  Northern Va. 1861-1865, 16th Va. Inf. CSA.

LOT 218
Ave. 4, Old 78
Owners - Robert Morton and Peele
Robert Edwin Epes - May 20, 1960, age 59 yrs.
Edna Morton Epes - Apr. 10, 1968 (vault).
Samuel Mahoney - buried Apr. 5, 1892, age 49 yrs.
M. A. Mahoney - buried Oct. 31, 1894, age 50 yrs.
Louise F. Peele Lucas - Feb. 24, 1914, age 71 yrs.
Miss Marion Morton - Sept. 10, 1939, age 74 yrs.
Miss Margaret Morton - Sept. 13, 1920, age 65 yrs.
Robert Morton - Apr. 11, 1899, age 85 yrs.
Charlotte Morton - July 9, 1894, age 68 yrs.

LOT 219
Ave. 3, Old 64

Owners - Cruise, Folger, Gordon and Dr. T. Sanford Cooke
Mary W. Cooke - June 28, 1951, age 55 yrs.
Thomas S. Cooke, M.D. - Nov. 15, 1953, age 72 yrs.
Catherine A. Gordon - Jan. 5, 1859, age 54 yrs.
Mrs. Ann Cruise - Jan. 29, 1867, age 80 yrs.
Mrs. Lydia Folger - Sept. 10, 1855, age 61 yrs. (yellow fever).
Constance E. Darden - June 25, 1908, age 12 yrs.

LOT 220
Ave. 4, Old 77
Owner - Welch
Annie V. Goodson - buried Aug. 1, 1893, age 18 yrs.
James Potter - 1822-1919, age 96 yrs., Engineer Corp. CSA.
Jeff D. Potter - Oct. 17, 1886, age 25 yrs.
Lucy Ann Potter - buried May 13, 1894.
Infant - stillborn, Apr. 14, 1886.

LOT 221
Ave. 3, Old 63
Owner - Stephen Skinner
Stephen Skinner - June 21, 1838, age 43 yrs.

LOT 222
Ave. 4, Old 76
Owners - N. and L. Owens
George Lee Phillips - July 27, 1863, age 1 yr.
Fannie Jennings Owens - Nov. 22, 1867, age 7 yrs.
Charles Pederick - May 24, 1870, age 10 yrs.
Thomas C. Owens - July 9, 1863, age 26 yrs., Co. G, Portsmouth
    Rifles, 9th Va., Regt. CSA.
Zachariah Owens - Jan. 7, 1875, age 79 yrs.
Fannie Toomer Owens - Nov. 12, 1872, age 77 yrs.
Mary Toomer Owens - Mar. 21, 1864, age 78 yrs.
Nathaniel Owens - Feb. 16, 1895, age 88 yrs.
James Toomer Owens - Apr. 19, 1835, age 7 yrs.
Fanny Toomer - Mar. 23, 1850, age 75 yrs.
William Fletcher Owens - Feb. 10, 1857, age 24 yrs.
Nathaniel Owens, Jr. - Apr. 1, 1861, age 20 yrs.

CEDAR GROVE CEMETERY
PLOT BOOK 2

LOT 224
Owner - Toomer
Charles O. Toomer - May 10, 1867, CSA.
Agnes Marie Toomer - Feb. 29, 1840, age 1 yr.
Fanny Toomer - June 30, 1870, age 62 yrs.
Note: May 12, 1829, James G. Toomer married Mrs. Fanny
Cherry, surety - William H. Wilson.

LOT 225
Ave. 3, Old 61
Owner - Thomas Forbes
Louisa C. Forbes - buried Feb. 28, 1890, age 74 yrs.
Elizabeth S. Forbes - buried June 7, 1892, age 48 yrs.
Thomas Forbes - 9th Va. Inf. CSA.

LOT 226
Ave. 3, Old 61
Owner - Butler
Harriet Ann Butler - died Sept. 15, 1837, age 2 yrs. 4 mos.
Catherine Butler - died July 5, 1843, age 32 yrs., wife of W. G.
Butler.
Note: Nov. 4, 1830, Willoughby G. Butler married Catherine
Forbes guardian, William Barnard, surety.

LOT 227
Ave. 3, Old 60
Owner - B. W. Jobson, N/H
Frank C. Armistead - died May 5, 1887, age 16 yrs.
Wiley Wallace Bush - died Oct. 3, 1914, age 45 yrs.
Leroy Lee Grant - died July 5, 1836, age 6 mos. 25 days.
Batson W. Jobson - 1804-1853.

Ebbytine Grant Jobson - 1809-1848.
Note: Oct. 1, 1829, Batson Jobson married Ebbyline Grant whose father, Edward Grant, was surety.

LOT 228
Ave. 4, Old 74
Owners - Singleton and Martin
Emma A. Singleton - died Sept. 16, 1855, age 27 yrs., (yellow fever).
Heber C. Cassell - died Mar. 8, 1936, age 73 yrs.
Marion M. Cassell - died Jan. 6, 1944, age 77 yrs.
Bessie M. Martin - 1890-1927, age 36 yrs.
Alexander Martin - died Jan. 22, 1954, age 64 yrs.
Sue H. Martin - Apr. 29, 1960, age 74 yrs.
Mary Louisa Singleton - died Oct. 13, 1831, age 4 yrs.
Sarah Francis Singleton - died July 27, 1824, age 12 yrs.
Ann Eliza Singleton - died Sept. 30, 1855, age 5 yrs., (yellow fever).
Mary Emma Singleton - died Sept. 13, 1855, age 6 yrs., (yellow fever).
Robert L. Martin - 1863-1920, age 37 yrs.
Rosalie Cassell Martin - died Aug. 3, 1962, age 91 yrs.
Rosalie C. Martin - died May 27, 1975, age 79 yrs.

LOT 229
Ave. 3, Old 60
Owner - Joseph Culpepper
Edith Culpepper - died Apr. 19, 1901, age 82 yrs.
Jesse Culpepper - died Nov. 11, 1873, age 57 yrs.
Joseph Culpepper - died Dec. 22, 1865, age 63 yrs.
Mary Eliza Culpepper - buried Nov. 7, 1887, age 6 yrs.
Charlie Shands Culpepper - died Jan. 20, 1879, age 28 yrs.
Lt. A. T. Culpepper - buried Nov. 1, 1894, age 64 yrs., 16th Va. Inf. CSA.

LOT 230
Ave. 4, Old 73
Owners - Robert Peed, Sallie Toomer, Moss Harmanson and Alice Moss Jones
Shelton Burton - buried Oct. 22, 1884, age 62 yrs.
William R. Burton - died Mar. 5, 1902, age 49 yrs.
Smith - stillborn, Aug. 30, 1889.
Sallie Toomer Moss Harmanson - Oct. 23, 1870 (vault).
Jane Peed Burton Moss - died May 30, 1912, age 75 yrs.
Sallie E. Burton - died Feb. 6, 1885, age 25 yrs.

Rev. Robert Peed - died June 14, 1866, age 64 yrs.
Mrs. Jane Peed - died Apr. 30, 1848, age 79 yrs.
Robert Peed, Esq. - died Oct. 14, 1840, age 69 yrs.
Sarah Frances Allen and infant Florence - died June 21, 1854, age 32 yrs.
William Herbert Burton - died 1849, age 54 yrs.
Sallie Herbert Toomer Burton - died Sept. 1, 1869, age 72 yrs.
Note: William H. Burton married Sarah Toomer, July 21, 1819, surety - Benjamim Rudd.

LOT 231
Ave. 3, Old 59
Owner - Mrs. Thomas Walter Mathews
Ernest Washington Lamons - Apr. 21, 1970 (vault). He was moved to Blacksburg, Va. on May 10, 1979.
Thomas Walter Mathews - Oct. 6, 1934, age 52 yrs.
Alice Rebecca Toomer Mathews - Sept. 6, 1969 (vault).
Monument - Erected by Petty Officers and Seamen of the USS Pennsylvania and Citizens of Portsmouth, Va., to Lt. William B. Lyne, United States Navy - died Apr. 29, 1841.
Note: June 10, 1829, William B. Lyne married Elizabeth S. Veale, whose mother, Elizabeth Veale, consents, surety - Samuel A. Browne. July 14, 1840, William B. Lyne married Mrs. Elizabeth B. Galt, surety - Samuel A. Browne.

LOT 232
Ave. 4, Old 72
Owner - James Reed
Note: This lot filled up completely. William (Bill) Morlino and Octavia Murdaugh, relatives of lot owner - Aug. 20, 1985.
1. Robert Carter Reed - died May 24, 1912, age 34 yrs.
2. Penbroke Reed - died Jan. 20, 1946, age 65 yrs.
3. Esther Reed - June 29, 1966, age 95 yrs.
4. Duncan Wood - died Jan. 26, 1942, age 65 yrs.
5. Margaret Reed Wood - buried Dec. 9, 1965.
6. Washington Reed - died Apr. 29, 1890, age 67 yrs., EM Dept. CSA.
7. Octavia Murdaugh Reed - died May 4, 1917, age 81 yrs.
8. Virginia C. Reed - 1819-1911, age 92 yrs.
9. James Reed - 1770-1854.
10. Esther Reed - 1788-1850.
11. Elizabeth T. Child - died Oct. 2, 1921, age 58 yrs.
12. Parrish - stillborn of C. T., Sept. 10, 1907.

LOT 233
Ave. 3, Old 58
Owner - Bagley
James Reed - died Mar. 12, 1942, age 80 yrs.
8 burial plots - no names.
Emily A. Bagley - buried July 4, 1890, age 64 yrs.
Lelia A. Bagley - died June 19, 1894, age 64 yrs.
Mary Eliza Cosetts - Feb. 7, 1905, age 58 yrs.

LOT 234
Ave. 4, Old 71
Owner - Dr. H. F. Butt
Warner M. Pugh - died Sept. 9, 1908, age 5 yrs.
Anna Mary Butt - died 1861.
Emily Susan Butt - died 1871.
Capt. W. R. Butt - CSN.
Adj. A. B. Butt - 41st Va. Inf. CSA.
Lt. D. A. Forrest - CSN.
Dr. Holt Fairfield Butt - died Oct. 9, 1900, age 65 yrs., Surgeon
   CSN.
Emily Susan Riddick Butt - died Mar. 2, 1917, age 80 yrs.
Mary H. Butt - died Apr. 7, 1842, age 18 yrs.
Nannie L. Page Butt - died Aug. 26, 1954, age 77 yrs.
Channing M. Butt - died June 13, 1904, age 59 yrs., CSA.
Effie Smith Butt - 1867-1892, age 25 yrs.
Robert B. Butt - died Oct. 16, 1908, age 28 yrs.
J. W. S. Butt, Jr. - buried Jan. 17, 189-, age 18 days.
Virginia Butt Watts - buried Oct. 15, 1893, age 10 mos.
Sarah B. Forrest - died June 14, 1887, age 56 yrs.
Mary E. Wilson - buried July 1, 1884, age 6 mos.
Note: Aug. 26, 1954 - Miss Nannie Louise Page Butt, age 77
   yrs., died this morning at Butt ancestral home North East
   corner of Crawford and Queen St. after a long illness. She
   was daughter of Dr. Holt Fairfield Butt and Emily Susan
   Riddick Butt. She was last surviving member of her family
   generation - funeral Trinity, burial Butt family plot Cedar
   Grove Cemetery, Portsmouth, Va. She was a Yeomonette in
   the Navy WWI, also in charge of Woodrow Wilson High
   School cafeteria since 1919.
      Survived by large group of nieces and nephews including:
   Mrs. Waverly R. Winborne, Mrs. Robert L. Nelson of Colum-
   bia, S.C., Mrs. H. F. Trotman, Jr., Mrs. J. Parrish Trant, Mrs.
   Wright Noble, Mrs. W. N. Watnough, Jr., of Baltimore, Md.,
   Alexander B. Butt, Jr., Marshall W. Butt, Bruce Wilcox Butt,
   Hope Wilson Butt, Sumner Riddick Pugh, H. F. B. Watts of

Raleigh, N.C., Col. Harry Lee Watts, USA, retired of Virginia Beach, Va.

LOT 235
Ave. 3, Old 57
Owner - Holt Wilson
Susan D. Wilson - buried Mar. 2, 1889, age 77 yrs.
L. Wilson - buried Apr. 23, 1897, age 72 yrs.
Columbia G. Wilson - buried Dec. 30, 1888, age 58 yrs.
Swempson Wilson - buried July 13, 1885, age 65 yrs.
Edwin N. Breuoorth - died Dec. 22, 1841, age 5 mos.
Louisana Wilson - died Apr. 25, 1897, age 74 yrs.
W. S. Wilson - 16th Va. Inf. CSA.
7 graves - no names.
Capt. H. Page - CSN.
Carter B. Page - buried Oct. 31, 1892, age 37 yrs.
Elizabeth P. Page - buried Mar. 1, 1894, age 78 yrs.
Edward J. Page - buried Apr. 29, 1894, age 36 yrs.
Note: Nov. 6, 1832 - Hugh Nelson Page married Mary Imogene Wheeler, consent of mother, Eliza N. Wheeler, states Hugh Nelson Page, Commander USN, witness to consent J. Schoolfield, surety - Thomas Williamson.

LOT 236
Ave. 5, Old 43
Owner - J. O. Shannon, S/H
Frank L. Shannon - died July 9, 1906, age 19 yrs.
Margaret L. Shannon - died Sept. 27, 1923, age 35 yrs.
James O. Shannon - died Dec. 16, 1940, age 79 yrs.
Lavinia T. Boush - died Mar. 11, 1887, age 46 yrs.
Laura V. Shannon - died Apr. 19, 1894, age 27 yrs.
Ethel D. Shannon - died May 22, 1894, age 3 mos.
James B. Shannon Morse - buried Apr. 5, 1972 (vault).

LOT 236
Ave. 5, Old 43
Owner - George W. Leigh
Hope T. Morse - Apr. 12, 1985 (vault).
Laura Shannon Lee Morse - May 4, 1973 (vault).
Willis Wray Morse, Sr. - May 16, 1974 (vault).
George W. Leigh - died July 19, 1895, age 52 yrs.
Rosa Leigh - died Oct. 7, 1910, age 65 yrs.
James S. Leigh - died Apr. 25, 1901, age 3 yrs. 4 mos.

LOT 237
Ave. 4, Old 42
Owner - W. J. Kellum, N/H
William J. Kellum - died Jan. 6, 1901, age 58 yrs.
Prestlow M. Miller - died Oct. 25, 1929, age 67 yrs.
Hazel Lee Kellum - buried Aug. 18, 1965.
Charles Kellum - died Nov. 1, 1885, age 11 yrs.
William Kellum - died Jan. 22, 1933, age 71 yrs.
Roberta Lee Kellum - Mar. 28, 1964.

LOT 238
Ave. 4, Old 42
Owners - Margaret Hargrove. Later - Willis Jenkins, S/H
Hargrove - stillborn, buried Mar. 8, 1889.
Mattie Dews Jenkins - 1868-1940, age 71 yrs.
Willis Asbury Jenkins - 1860-1929.
Jule Dews Jenkins - 1898-1927.
Margaret A. Hargroves or Hargraves - 1819-1887, age 67 yrs.
Willis A. Jenkins, Jr. - 1897-1899, age 2 yrs.

LOT 239
Ave. 4, Old 41
Owner - W. C. Corbitt or Corbett
Henry R. Garrett - Ret. SAL Railroad, sister Mrs. May Garrett
    Wilson Montrose, Va., Westmoreland, Va.
William B. Corbett - June 10, 1887, age 2 yrs.
Elizabeth Corbett - 1829-1905, age 76 yrs.
Johnson Corbett - 1832-1859, age 10 yrs. (This must not be
    correct.)
Willie Corbett - 1887-1887.
Lizzie Corbett - 1881-1881.
J. Etta Corbett - 1859-1860.
Lizzie E. Corbett - 1856-1866, age 9 yrs.
Nannie B. Corbett - 1857-1903, age 46 yrs.
William Corbett - 1854-1922, age 62 yrs.
Annie Garrett - died Jan. 2, 1950, age 83 yrs.
Rev. Richard Baynham Garrett - 1854-1922, age 67 yrs.

LOT 240
Ave. 5, Old 44
Owner - R. E. Hawks, N/H
Sarah Cato Renn - died Aug. 22, 1904, age 1 yr.
Lt. R. E. Hawks, buried Dec. 22, 1888, age 53 yrs., CSA.
Otis Drewry Hawks - died Feb. 23, 1910, age 37 yrs.
Martha Lillian Renn - died Mar. 23, 1907, age 1 yr.

Hawks - stillborn, Nov. 9, 1901.
Susan P. Hawks - died June 11, 1910, age 66 yrs.
Archie A. Hawks - died May 10, 1921, age 52 yrs.

LOT 240
Ave. 5, Old 44
Owner - Clara Grace Codd, S/H
Charles Porter - buried Oct. 7, 1892, age 3 yrs.
Mary A. Codd - died May 24, 1884.
John A. Codd, Sr. - died May 17, 1874.
Clara Grace Codd - died Sept. 14, 1902, age 73 yrs.
Kate Maude Codd Porter - died Nov. 28, 1905, age 36 yrs.

LOT 241
Ave. 4, Old 40
Owner - Mary A. Anderson
Laural Palmer Anderson - May 28, 1900, age 21 yrs.
Laura Kathleen Anderson - died June 20, 1900, age 1 yr. 5 mos.
Mary Virginia Wise Anderson - died Mar. 13, 1914, age 63 yrs.
Harman Anderson - died June 14, 1927, age 83 yrs.
Mary R. Anderson - died Apr. 11, 1956, age 72 yrs.

LOT 242 W
E. Ave. 5
Owner - Reverdy Jones
1. Reverdy H. Jones - died Dec. 13, 1959, age 78 yrs.
2. Sophie Nash Benson Jones - buried Nov. 9, 1972 (vault).
3. Reverdy H. Jones, Jr. - buried June 7, 1980 (cremains).
4, 7, 8, 9. - Empty.
5. Thomas C. Nash - died July 21, 1951, age 68 yrs.
6. Elizabeth B. Nash - died Sept. 24, 1953, age 71 yrs.
10. Stone. John E. Anderson - Aug. 19, 1977 (cremains).
11. Stone. Eugenia Nash Anderson - Feb. 23, 1984 (cremains),
   reinterred Jan. 28, 1985.

LOT 243
Ave. 4, Old 39
Owner - Virginius Butt
Oast - stillborn, Jan. 24, 1926.
William Perkins - Feb. 4, 1943, age 77 yrs.
Lela Perkins - June 17, 1967 (vault).
Monument
Sallie Francis Butt - May 10, 1924, age 72 yrs.
Virginius Butt - Nov. 11, 1898, age 50 yrs.
Sadie H. Butt - Dec. 16, 1956, age 82 yrs.

LOT 244
Ave. 5, Old 46
Owner - R. J. Neely
John Neely - Nov. 18, 1968 (vault).
Fartunal McCrow Neely - died Mar. 30, 1962, age 71 yrs.
Emily Goodwyn Neely - died Mar. 15, 1910, age 19 yrs.
Louise Blunt Neely - died Mar. 17, 1918, age 1 yr. 5 mos.
Elizabeth N. Ridley Neely - died Aug. 7, 1924, age 77 yrs.
Robert Johnson Neely - died Dec. 5, 1890, age 63 yrs., CSA.
William Ridley Neely - died Apr. 11, 1916, age 43 yrs.
Clara Johnson Neely - Mar. 31, 1964, age 93 yrs.
Note: 1900 Census - Portsmouth, Va., Elizabeth N. Ridley
Neely, born Va., Parents born Va. Children: Eliza, Feb. 1874,
Jane B., Feb. 1878, Robert J., Feb. 1879, Emily, Oct. 1890,
John Thompson, Feb. 1883.
Obit.: Portsmouth, Va. Died Mar. 31, 1964, Miss Clara
Johnson Neely, age 93, retired Missionary to Japan, daughter
of Robert Johnson and Elizabeth Ridley Neely, native of
Portsmouth.
One of the first Missionary sent to Japan by Episcopal
Church, 1899, served Tokyo and Kyoto for 35 years, retired
1934, she lived 504 North St. and taught Bible Study at
Trinity Church. Survived by brother J. Thompson Neely of
Norfolk. Brennan Funeral Home was in charge, buried
Cedar Grove.

LOT 245
Ave. 4, Old 38
Owner - H. F. Butt, Jr.
Leonora Wilcox Butt - Jan. 12, 1974.
H. Fairfield Butt, Jr. - died Aug. 23, 1936, age 75 yrs.
Henry J. Wilcox - 1857-1918.
Emma Luella Wilcox - buried Apr. 1, 1946.

LOT 246
Ave. 5, Old 47
Owners - John Y. Robinson, S/H - Leon F. Jones, N/H
John Y. Robinson - died Dec. 24, 1937, age 59 yrs.
Sallie S. Robinson - died Sept. 27, 1956, age 83 yrs.
Laura Stewart Jones - Sept. 17, 1916, age 7 yrs.
Sarah S. Jones - Aug. 15, 1837, age 55 yrs.
Leon F. Jones - Jan. 2, 1936, age 66 yrs.

LOT 247
Ave. 5, Old 48, East End
Owner - Stephen Bowers
Mary D. Whitehurst - died June 21, 1905, age 5 mos.
Josephine E. Whitehurst - died Mar. 6, 1912, age 16 yrs.
May Bowers Whitehurst - died Apr. 27, 1929.
Josephine Bowers - died Aug. 27, 1949, age 86 yrs.
William D. Bowers - died Mar. 21, 1948, age 92 yrs.
Jane Veal Denby - died Dec. 12, 1856.
Blanch Bowers - died Oct. 22, 1918, age 52 yrs.
Adelia Denby Bowers - died May 26, 1884, age 19 yrs.
Mary Jane Bowers - died Dec. 30, 1912, age 81 yrs.
Stephen Bowers - died Mar. 18, 1919, age 89 yrs.
Mahaly M. Bowers - died Aug. 8, 1855.

LOT 247
Ave. 4, Old 48, West End
Owner - Stephen Bowers
Jane Demby - removed from Portlock to Cedar Grove.
Shirley Dashiell - died Aug. 25, 1906, age 3 yrs. 7 mos.
Shirley Dashiell
James Clifton Dashiell - Jan. 6, 1964.
Eva Bowers Dashiell - died Apr. 1961, age 90 yrs.
Edward W. Dashiell - 1874-1920, age 45 yrs.

LOT 248
Ave. 5, Old 49
Owner - W. L. D. Virnelson
Clarence W. Peed - Aug. 23, 1970 (vault).
W. L. D. Virnelson - buried Dec. 10, 1893, age 56 yrs.
Adelia Denby Virnelson - buried May 26, 1889, age 45 yrs.
Thomas Clarence Peed - died Oct. 26, 1921, age 54 yrs.
Mamie V. Peed - died Sept. 23, 1932, age 66 yrs.

LOT 249
Ave. 10
Owner - John Burke
John Burke - died Nov. 29, 1878, age 87 yrs.
John H. Gregory - died Oct. 29, 1865.
Eliza Nee Burke Gregory - died June 10, 1888.
Monument
Eliza Burke - Aug. 30, 1840.
John H. Gregory, Jr. - died Jan. 18, 1864, age 15 yrs.
Note: Apr. 24, 1821 - John Burke married Eliza Keenan, surety
  - Barnard O'Neill.

LOT 250
Ave. 10, Old M
Owner - Thomas W. Godwin
James W. Godwin - Oct. 17, 1907, age 24 yrs.
Margaret G. Scott - Sept. 29, 1906, age 20 yrs.
James T. Godwin - Oct. 1, 1896, age 40 yrs.
Emma S. Godwin - Sept. 29, 1892, age 36 yrs.
Mary Waler Godwin - age 3 mos.
Frank Thomas Godwin - infant.
Indiana Godwin - June 17, 1909, age 75 yrs.
Thomas W. Godwin - Sept. 4, 1907, age 74 yrs.
Mary F. Godwin - Sept. 30, 1880, age 11 yrs.
Margaret E. Godwin - July 18, 1866, age 29 yrs.
Mary A. Whiting - Apr. 3, 1887 or 1879.
Maurice K. Taylor - Apr. 9, 1893, age 52 yrs. 9 mos.

LOT 251
Ave. 10, Old 1
Owner - Thomas Webb
William F. Taylor - Dec. 19, 1914, age 47 yrs.
Annie W. Marchant - Feb. 22, 1931, age 62 yrs.
Robert William Webb - 1863-1923, age 59 yrs.
Florence G. Webb - 1871-1940, age 68 yrs.
Maxwell Webb - 1903-1914, age 11 yrs.
2 graves - no names.
Thomas Howard Webb - 1822-1880, age 57 yrs.
Mary Elizabeth Webb - 1830-1917, age 86 yrs.
Harriett C. Smith - July 26, 1854, age 23 yrs.
George A. Smith - Oct. 5, 1867, age 34 yrs.
James Walter Webb - Sept. 14, 1898, age 48 yrs.

LOT 252
Ave. 10, Old K
Owner - Daniel Gaskins
William Dorsey Pruden - Sept. 24, 1903, age 11 yrs.
Julius H. Gaskins - died May 23, 1887, age 41 yrs.
J. H. Trotter - stillborn, buried Oct. 22, 1902.
Webster D. Gaskins - died Aug. 25, 1889, age 5 yrs. 9 mos.
Capt. B. Frank Vaughan
Georgia A. Vaughan - 1848-1931, age 83 yrs.
Lerox Frank Vaughan - Jan. 26, 1966.
Louisa Journee Vaughan - Aug. 10, 1974.
M. D. Gaskins - Sept. 11, 1897, age 6 yrs.
D. W. Gaskins - Nov. 12, 1891, age 32 yrs.

Alteria M. Gaskins - July 20, 1925, age 64 yrs.
Julia A. V. Gaskins - Jan. 28, 1906, age 85 yrs.

LOT 253
Ave. 10, Old J
Owner - W. B. Collins
Charles A. Couper - Jan. 16, 1901, age 8 yrs. 6 mos.
C. Couper - May 30, 1912, age 71 yrs., 16th Va. Inf. CSA.
Elizabeth Collins Couper - 1838-1934, age 96 yrs.
Charles Ashton - June 24, 1948, age 81 yrs.
Wills Cowper - Aug. 30, 1906, age 51 yrs.
Louisa J. Collins - Feb. 12, 1912, age 85 yrs.
Lucy Ashton Couper - June 28 (no year), age 76 yrs. 4 mos.
W. W. Collins - 16th Va. Inf. CSA.
C. W. Collins - 61st Va. Inf. CSA.
Stillborn - Oct. 2, 1889 (no name).
Note: Dec. 27, 1827 - William B. Collins married Lucy Ann
    Watts, ward of said William Collins, surety - David Jarvis.

LOT 254
Ave. 10, Old 1
Owner - Joseph Moore
E. M. Moore - Signal Corp, CSA.
James H. Warner - age 24 yrs., Chief Engineer, CSN.
Mary Johnston Moore - Aug. 11, 1911, age 74 yrs.
Capt. John William Moore - Jan. 22, 1891, age 59 yrs., CSA.
Major J. H. Warner - Jan. 5, 1885, CSA.
Mary Frances Moore - buried Apr. 25, 1927.
Moved from Old Glasgow St. Cemetery.
Frances Marion Moore - Sept. 2, 1893, age 47 yrs.
Caroline N. Porter Moore - Sept. 29, 1887, age 78 yrs.
Joseph Moore - Oct. 25, 1861, age 54 yrs.
Mary Frances Moore - Oct. 11, 1832, age 3 yrs.
Percy McAlpine Moore - Feb. 26, 1874, infant.
Forrest Newton Moore - Apr. 17, 1880, 1878-1880.
Joseph Porter Moore - July 11, 1882, age 45 yrs., 9th Va. Inf.
    CSA.
Mary Elizabeth Moore - died Sept. 15, 1913, age 68 yrs.
Minnie Lee Moore - died May 23, 1949, age 81 yrs.
May Beverly Moore - died May 4, 1909, age 3 mos.

LOT 255
Old H
Owner - G. W. O. Maupin
Edward S. Maupin - May 5, 1982, age 65 yrs. (vault).

Edward W. Maupin, Jr. - June 11, 1959, age 82 yrs.
Marjorie Watts Maupin - Apr. 27, 1969 (vault).
Mary Wilson Maupin - July 4, 1921, age 76 yrs.
George W. O. Maupin, M.D. - Sept. 17, 1912, age 67 yrs.
Margaret Murdaugh Maupin - May 17, 1892, age 20 yrs.
Mary W. Pillmore - Mar. 13, 1945.
Ida Adair Maupin - Oct. 31, 1889, age 2 yrs.
Sallie C. M. Maupin - July 11, 1948, age 93 yrs.
Ann W. Maupin Bidgood - 1852-1935, age 83 yrs.
George W. O. Maupin, Sr., M.D. - 1822-1888, age 66 yrs.
Ann Augusta Maupin - 1823-1889, age 66 yrs.
Ada Augusta Maupin - 1863-1887, age 23 yrs.
William H. A. Maupin - 1859-1900, age 41 yrs.
John Cocke Maupin - May 19, 1889, age 38 yrs.
Note: Virginia Pilot - June 12, 1959. E. W. (Ned) Maupin, Jr.,
former City Councilman, retired Sec./Treas. Portsmouth
Lumber Company, City Council May 1925-Sept. 1932, died
Thursday, Portsmouth Hospital.
Husband of Mrs. Marjorie Watts Maupin, 516 North St.,
son of the late Edward Watts and Mrs. Ebbieline Brown
Maupin. Founder of scouting program in Portsmouth, First
President Portsmouth Boy Scouts 1920 when it was organ-
ized. Received Antelope Award for distinguished service to
boyhood. Council top award "Silver Beaver." He was survived by son, Edward Samuel Maupin, of Richmond, Va.;
daughter, Mrs. R. E. Bruce Stewart, Jr., of Portsmouth; 3
grandsons: R. E. Bruce Stewart III, Edward Maupin Stewart
of Portsmouth, Edward Samuel Maupin, Jr., of Richmond,
Va. Burial Cedar Grove, Foster Funeral Home in charge.

LOT 256
Ave, 5, Old 163
Owner - E. C. Brooks
Bill Brooks Briggs - Dec. 10, 1924, age 56 yrs.
Frank Thomas Briggs - June 30, 1931, age 64 yrs.
Carrie Briggs - Dec. 4, 1951.
Joseph D. Robertson - Oct. 18, 1918, age 46 yrs.
E. C. Brooks - Nov. 1, 1910, age 74 yrs.
Haseltine Brooks - June 5, 1890, age 56 yrs.
J. Sherwood - 61st Va. Inf. CSA.
Engr. William Brockett - CSA.
Harwood Briggs - died June 22, 1904, age 10 mos.
Ann H. Brooks - buried June 11, 1890, age 57 yrs.
Brooks C. Briggs - buried July 1, 1895, age 9 mos.

LOT 257
Ave. 4, Old 167 P
Owners - L. R. Watts, N/H - David Griffith, S/H
Ann M. Watts - died Oct. 9, 1961, age 88 yrs.
Wenifred Brown - died Apr. 3, 1959, age 76 yrs.
William Ambrose Brown - July 14, 1965 (vault).
Samuel Watts - 1876-1911, age 34 yrs.
Martha Peters Watts - 1848-1934, age 86 yrs.
Leigh Richmond Watts - 1843-1919, age 76 yrs., Signal Corps
    CSA.
David Griffith
Prudence Griffith
Note: Mar. 16, 1826 - David Griffith married Almira Elizabeth
    Clements, guardian, Robert B. Butt, surety.
      Jan. 14, 1836 - David Griffith married Prudence T. Mof-
    fatt, surety - John P. Young.

LOT 258
Ave. 5, Old 162
Owner - William H. Brown, N/H
William H. Brown - Nov. 21, 1911, age 76 yrs.
Joseph C. Brown - May 26, 1921, age 76 yrs.
Sarah Ann Brown - buried May 31, 1892, age 53 yrs.
Alice V. Brown - buried Apr. 23, 1886, age 24 yrs.
George B. Brown - buried July 15, 1886, age 10 mos.
B. E. Ricketts - buried May 10, 1897, age 3 mos.
William Joseph Ricketts - June 29, 1905, age 2 yrs. 11 mos.
Jesse E. Ricketts - June 22, 1905, age 16 mos.
Simmonds - stillborn, June 21, 1935.
Annie Bessie Ricketts - Feb. 4, 1972 (vault).
Corp. Elijah Ricketts - died Dec. 30, 1932, age 60 yrs., Co. L2,
    Va. Inf. Spanish American War.

LOT 259
Ave. 4, Old 166
Owner - Thomas Brooks
Henry Watson Brooks - 1846-1888, age 42 yrs.
James Madison Brooks - 1856-1905, age 49 yrs.
Edward F. Brooks - died May 20, 1947, age 85 yrs.
Julis Fritts Brooks - 1849-1914, age 65 yrs.
Thomas Brooks - 1818-1862, age 43 yrs.
Thomas Brooks, Jr. - 1851-1861, age 10 yrs.
Julia A. Brooks - 1820-1890, age 70 yrs.
Mrs. Mary Dickson - Mar. 23, 1810, age 28 yrs.
William Davis - May 21, 1808, age 28 yrs.

Debra Davis - died July 3 1808, age 30 yrs.
Tudor Frith Brooks - died Apr. 22, 1911, age 70 yrs., Pvt. O. D. Guards., CSA.
Capt. John M. Foster - died Dec. 7, 1852, age 66 yrs.
Mrs. Sarah Foster - 1798-1874, age 75 yrs.
Charles Lee Brooks - 1859-1895, age 35 yrs.
T. F. Brooks - Apr. 18, 1911, age 70 yrs.
Note: Apr. 4, 1818 - John M. Foster married Sarah Brooks, surety - Smith Sherwood, guardian of Sarah.
   Dec. 2, 1840 - Thomas Brooks, Jr. married Julia Ann Frith, guardian William Benthall, surety.

LOT 260
Ave. 5, Old 162
Owners - Thomas Roberts - Sarah Roberts Brown, sister, S / H
Sergent H. F. Roberts - May 26, 1898, age 61 yrs.
Couper C. Roberts - Oct. 15, 1893, age 3 yrs.
Virginia Jackson Peck - Aug. 19, 1923, age 56 yrs.
Jethro Peck - Mar. 30, 1917, age 62 yrs.
Hattie Estelle Waller - Nov. 14, 1901, age 8 yrs.
Emma Roberts - Nov. 4, 1936, age 75 yrs.
Sarah F. Roberts - May 25, 1898, age 62 yrs.
Emma Virginia Waller - Feb. 1, 1892, age 2 yrs.

LOT 261
Ave. 4, Old 165
Owner - William H. Spooner
Eveline Spooner Shultz - died Dec. 6, 1928, age 80 yrs.
Romarza Spooner - died 1842.
Elizabeth Spooner - Apr. 12, 1887, age 73 yrs.
William H. Spooner - died Jan. 21, 1888, age 81 yrs.
Note: Mar. 18, 1830 - William H. Spooner married Eveline S. Bidgood, surety - John Dean.

LOT 262
Ave. 5, Old 161
Owner - H. F. Young
Miss J. Young - June 12, 1918, age 84 yrs.
Lula Cuga - buried July 1, 1890, age 24 yrs.

LOT 263
Ave. 4, Old 165
Owner - George Pulson, S / H
6 burial spaces - no names found.

LOT 264
Ave. 5, Old 160
Owner - Henry Allen
Henry L. Allen - Sept. 1, 1912, age 45 yrs.
John C. Woodley - Sept. 20, 1912, age 55 yrs.
Ida Allen Woodley - Oct. 12, 1943, age 84 yrs.
Elizabeth Garland Allen - Apr. 19, 1964, age 89 yrs.
Lucy Allen Woodley - Aug. 22, 1973.
Sarah Nash Woodley - Aug. 17, 1976 (vault).
Carrie Ross Pearson - Apr. 10, 1882, age 6 yrs.
Capt. H. A. Allen - died July 7, 1912, age 80 yrs., 9th Va. Inf.
   CSA.
Sarah Anne Allen - May 9, 1919, age 85 yrs.
Lucy M. Allen - June 9, 1889, age 27 yrs.

LOT 265
Ave. 4, Old 164
Owner - John L. Langhorne
J. L. Langhorne - CSN.
Fannie E. Hill Langhorne - May 5, 1905, age 60 yrs.
James K. Langhorne - Apr. 12, 1810, age 70 yrs., CSA.
Julia Langhorne - Jan. 13, 1951, age 70 yrs.
Lt. J. H. Robinson - buried Dec. 14, 1890, age 49 yrs., 9th Va.
   Inf. CSA.
Mary E. Robinson - buried May 24, 1894, age 61 yrs.
Note: Sept. 18, 1832 - James H. Langhorne married Mary R.
   King, surety - James Murdaugh.

LOT 266
Ave. 5, Old 182
Owner - Charles E. Cassell
William R. Berkley - Dec. 26, 1920, age 43 yrs.
Charles Emmett Cassell - died Aug. 29, 1816, age 77 yrs., 1st Lt.
   Engineer Corps. CSA.
Sallie Winifred Cassell - died July 1, 1879.
John F. S. Cassell - died Oct. 2, 1909, age 37 yrs.
Mary Virginia Cassell - Oct. 22, 1945, age 74 yrs.
Mattie C. Chiles - died June 30, 1962, age 86 yrs.
Richard T. Chiles - died June 4, 1957, age 75 yrs.
Charles E. Cassell, Jr. - July 27, 1876.
Helen Cassell - July 27, 1878.
Premrose Cassell Berkeley - Nov. 18, 1967.
Mary Berkley DeMurguiondo - Apr. 13, 1977 (reserved for her).

LOT 267
Ave. 4, Old 181
Owners - Wilkins and Wright
Mary Ethel Wright - Jan. 18, 1929, age 47 yrs.
Julia E. Wright - May 19, 1899, age 4 mos.
Frank D. Wright - May 4, 1904, age 5 mos.
James H. Finley - buried Nov. 4, 1888, age 1 yr. 1 mo.
George T. Wright - Dec. 16, 1933, age 80 yrs.
Mary S. Wright - Sept. 17, 1921, age 62 yrs.
Florence Wright - May 15, 1904, age 2 mos.
Wright - stillborn of George and Mary Wright, Dec. 19, 1905.
18 burial spaces - only 9 names.

LOT 268
Ave. 5, Old U
Owner - A. N. Longhridge or Laughridge, N/H
Alonzo N. Longhridge - Dec. 23, 1903, age 68 yrs.
Margaret L. Longhridge - Jan. 4, 1948, age 86 yrs.

LOT 269
Ave. 4, Old 180
Owners - Jacob J. Williams and George Williams, N/H
Jacob H. William
E. T. Summers - Grimes Bat. CSA.
Lucy Ida Williams
George Williams
Eliza Barron Williams - buried Dec. 1, 1890, age 86 yrs.
Jacob Jordan Williams - buried Jan. 11, 1885, age 73 yrs.
Franklin N. Williams

LOT 270
Ave. 5, Old U
Owner - William C. Bryson, S/H
William C. Bryson - Aug. 23, 1830-Feb. 13, 1893, age 63 yrs.
Rosalie Bryson - July 15, 1833-Feb. 9, 1910, age 78 yrs.
Martha M. Bryson - Dec. 28, 1856-Mar. 6, 1928, age 73 yrs.
Monument
Note: In my book of cemetery inscriptions, I have James Rike
    listed with this family. James Rike died July 5, 1852, age 49
    yrs.

LOT 271
Ave. 4, Old 180
Owner - William Hanrahan
Ellen F. Hanrahan - died Apr. 3, 1888, age 60 yrs.

James Pike - died July 5, 1852, age 49 yrs.
4 graves - no names.

LOT 272
Ave. 5, Old T2
Owner - U. B. Bilisoly
Urbain B. Bilisoly - died Aug. 20, 1914, age 74 yrs., Old Dominion Guard, Co. K, 9th Va. CSA.
Elizabeth Hodges Bilisoly - Mar. 1, 1911, age 66 yrs.
Virginia Bilisoly - Jan. 26, 1948, age 64 yrs.
Eugene E. Bilisoly - Sept. 9, 1890, age 46 yrs., Sergt. 9th Va. Inf. CSA.
Rosa Bilisoly - Apr. 1, 1952, age 79 yrs.
Adolphus J. Bilisoly - died July 25, 1887, age 45 yrs., Sergt. 9th Va. Inf. CSA.

LOT 273
Ave. 4, Old 225
Owner - Joseph P. Reynolds
Gerard Henderson - July 29, 1865.
Mrs. Jermima Reynolds - Oct. 19, 1874, age 71 yrs.
Joseph P. Reynolds - Dec. 20, 1858, age 53 yrs.
Robert Emmett Reynolds - June 12, 1864, Norfolk L.A.B. CSA.
Virginia Isabella Henderson - Sept. 20, 1855, age 13 yrs. (yellow fever).
James Reynolds - Oct. 4, 1855, age 7 yrs. (yellow fever).
Gerard Irwin Henderson - Aug. 8, 1862, age 4 yrs.
Monument: Mary J. Henderson - buried Nov. 8, 1884, age 60 yrs.
Charles V. Jordan - Feb. 11, 1914, age 75 yrs.
Josephine H. Jordan - Sept. 1, 1923, age 79 yrs.
Emily Godwin Jordan - buried Dec. 25, 1898, age 2 yrs.
Note: Dec. 24, 1840 - Joseph P. Reynolds married Mrs. Jemima Ellis, surety - Gerard Henderson.
Dec. 24, 1840 - Gerard Henderson married Mary Jane Walls whose mother Jemima Ellis consents, witness to consent Thomas Reynolds, surety - Joseph P. Reynolds.

LOT 274
Ave. 5, Old T1
Owner - John L. Thomas
Cornelius Thomas - 1853-1933, age 79 yrs.
Chessie M. A. Thomas - Feb. 2, 1960 (vault).
John L. Thomas - June 25, 1985 (vault).
Sallie E. Thomas - Nov. 18, 1855-Jan. 16, 1879, age 24 yrs.

Rose Thomas Menger - May 7, 1869-May 27, 1909, age 40 yrs.
Alice Virginia Thomas - May 27, 1857.
Sallie E. Thomas - June 1, 1879.

LOT 275
Ave. 4, Old O
Owner - John L. Thomas
Mary F. Thomas - Aug. 9, 1899, age 72 yrs.
John L. Thomas - Sept. 3, 1898, age 71 yrs.
Monument

LOT 276
Ave. 5, Old T
Owner - Charles D. Pedrick
Samuel D. Pedrick - Dec. 24, 1945, age 67 yrs.
Rufus W. Brooks - 1864-1923, age 58 yrs.
Mary Dreurey Pedrick Brooks - Nov. 25, 1938, age 67 yrs.
Mrs. Ann Dreurey - Apr. 12, 1876, age 77 yrs.
Emma L. Pedrick - 1873-1912, age 39 yrs.
Charles William Pedrick - died Aug. 5, 1880, Medical Corps.
    CSA.
Mary F. Owens Pedrick - May 3, 1895, age 56 yrs.

LOT 277
Ave. 4, Old O
Owner - Rev. Vernon Eskridge
Sarah E. White - Jan. 22, 1922, age 61 yrs.
Sarah E. White - June 16, 1930, age 89 yrs.
Lt. William H. White - July 1 1862, age 26 yrs., Co. G, 9th Va.
    Regt. Va. Volunteers CSA.
Rev. Vernon Eskridge - Sept. 11, 1855 (yellow fever), Chaplain
    USN.
Monument

LOT 278
Ave. 5, Old S
Owners - John Gayle N/3/5 - John J. Carr S/2/5
John J. Carr - Mar. 17, 1907, age 73 yrs.
Jennie V. C. Carr - Jan. 20, 1899, age 58 yrs.
Dr. Edward Maupin Gayle - June 22, 1938, age 61 yrs.
Edward Nichols Wilcox - 1850-1901.
Margaret Downing Wilcox - 1851-1929, age 77 yrs.
Cora W. Hunter - Nov. 7, 1942, age 70 yrs.
Frank S. McDowell - July 21, 1957, age 53 yrs.
Capt. J. Gayle - July 6, 1884, age 48 yrs., 16th Va. Inf. CSA.

Mrs. Cora Wilcox Gayle - Oct. 26, 1889, age 43 yrs.
Julius H. Wilcox - Dec. 19, 1892, age 40 yrs.
Elizabeth Obeirne - infant, Oct. 30, 1944.
Elizabeth Obeirne - Aug. 18, 1943.

LOT 279
Ave. 4, Old 202
Owner - Jordan Curlin
Annie Hope Richardson - 1882-1886, age 3 yrs.
Norman W. Richardson - 1890-1900, age 9 yrs.
Elizabeth Curlin White - 1832-1861, age 28 yrs.
Jordan Curlin - Sept. 30, 1855, age 55 yrs. (yellow fever).
Ann A. Curlin - Sept. 21, 1855, age 46 yrs. (yellow fever).
William F. Richardson - 1888-1909, age 21 yrs.
Mrs. Florence Richardson - Aug. 16, 1938, age 82 yrs.
Joseph B. Richardson - 1851-1900, age 48 yrs.
Susie Garson Hickman - June 24, 1943, age 73 yrs.
Willie F. Hickman - 1863-1933, age 70 yrs.
Annie L. Crismond - Dec. 8, 1932, age 85 yrs.
Monument

LOT 280
Ave. 5, Old R
Owners - Aylwin and Watson
No interment found in records.
Note: Aylwin family died 1855, yellow fever, member Saint
Pauls Catholic Church. The father, Matthew W. Aylwin was
born in England and died in Brooklyn, New York, at age 78
yrs. and 7 mos., Oct. 4, 1881. The yellow fever death records
for summer 1855 list Mrs. M. W. Aylwin and son of Mrs. M.
W. Aylwin.

LOT 281
Ave. 4, Old 201
Owner - George Marshall
George Marshall - Aug. 2, 1855, age 74 yrs., Gunner USN.
Phillip Marshall - age 79 yrs.
Sophia City - 1808-1877, age 69 yrs.
George J. Marshall - Nov. 10, 1847, age 22 yrs.
Samuel City - 1797-1860, age 63 yrs.
Sophia Eugenia City - Apr. 5, 1849, age 9 yrs. 4 mos.
George Marshall Sirian - July 24, 1841, age 4 mos.
Jane Higgs - Sept. 2, 1839, age 74 yrs.
Mary Ann Higgs - Aug. 6, 1855, age 47 yrs. (yellow fever).
Note: Jan. 25, 1835 - Samuel City married Sophia Marshall,

surety - Benjamin Crow.

Apr. 29, 1840 - George Sirian married Eleanor Marshall, her father, George Marshall, consents, wit to consent, William W. Davis.

LOT 282
Ave. 5, Old V
Owner - C. A. Forbes, N/H
C. A. Forbes - buried Mar. 7, 1898, age 78 yrs.
Harman H. Richardson - Aug. 24, 1908, age 70 yrs.
H. F. Woodhouse - buried Mar. 28, 1896, age 75 yrs.
E. Mary Maude Forbes - Jan. 18, 1955, age 89 yrs.

LOT 283
Ave. 4, Old 179
Owner - George James, M.D.
Note: No burials made unless approved by Rosa L. Wooten, daughter of Clarence.
Mattie Virnelson - Jan. 5, 1891.
Clarence R. Hunt - Sept. 14, 1912, age 2 mos.
Rosa Lee Wooten - Jan. 4, 1985 (vault).
Stephen C. James, Jr. - Jan. 5, 1912, buried Jan. 6, 1912, age 81 yrs.
Alta B. James - June 7, 1903.
George James, M.D. - 1844.
Samuel W. K. Wooten - July 25, 1951, age 57 yrs.
Jennett J. James - 1806-1847, age 40 yrs. 11 mos.
Stephen J. James - Grimes Battery CSA.
Note: Jan. 4, 1826 - Stephen James married Jennett Mackie, father, George Mackie, surety.

LOT 284
Ave. 5, Old V
Owner - Cornelius Forbes, S/H
Mary Ann Hoffman - buried Dec. 10, 1890, age 88 yrs.
Harry Forbes Wood - Jan. 17, 1904, age 28 yrs.
William Howard Tilson - June 5, 1904, age 3 mos.
Catherine J. Forbes - June 11, 1914, age 48 yrs.
Emory Wood - June 1, 1943, age 60 yrs.

LOT 285
Ave. 4, Old 178
Owners - Neston Richardson, N/H - N. S. Forbes, S/H
Miss Marie Louise Thacker - June 6, 1939, age 73 yrs.
Josephine Hutchens - died Sept. 24, 1941, age 62 yrs.

Neston R. Goodman - 1906-1933, age 27 yrs.
N. S. Forbes - 1813-1876.
Rhoda Forbes - 1817-1876.
Julia Forbes - 1841-1843.
E. V. White - 1839-1919, age 79 yrs., CSN.
Monument - E. V. White - Asst. Engnr. Merrimac 1861-1865 Virginia.
Antoinette Thacker Richardson - 1847-1928, age 81 yrs.
Neston F. Richardson - age 75 yrs., Signal Corp CSA 1840 1916.
Josephine Forbes White - 1838-1895, age 57 yrs.
Note: Norfolk Co., May 16, 1837 - Nathan S. Forbes married Rhoda McCoy, father, Josiah McCoy.
    News Paper 1919: Capt. E. V. White of Swimming Point, Portsmouth, who in 1862 was engineer aboard the CSS Virginia (Merrimac) when it fought the USS Monitor in Hampton Roads, died of heart attack at Clifton Springs, N.Y. Capt. White was 79 yrs. of age, native of Ga., he came to Portsmouth, Va., outbreak of war between the states. After the destruction of Merrimac, Capt. White went to Columbus, Ga. and manufactured all the buttons used by the CSA. He was commissioned CSA and was wounded by a sword of Federal Officer. After war, he returned to Portsmouth and went into business. E. V. White & Co., dealers in Railroad and Steamship Supplies. Founder 1893, Portsmouth Park View Methodist Church. Present church was erected 1924-25 from base funds he left.

LOT 286
Ave. 5, Old 184
Owner - James E. Wilson, N/H
Louisa P. Danco - July 6, 1972 (vault).
John W. Paxson - 1870-1919, age 48 yrs.
Elizabeth Hilda Young Paxson (or Parson) - Apr. 4, 1939, age 79 yrs.
Frances Parker - July 11, 1849 age 33 yrs.
Indiana C. Young - June 16, 1945, age 78 yrs.
Mary Lawson Young - Dec. 1 1938, age 77 yrs.

LOT 287
Ave. 5, Old 184
Owner - James E. Wilson, S/H
Mary Frances Wilson - Nov. 11, 1813, age 35 yrs.
Reinter remains from sea Wilson - Apr. 18, 1972.
M. William Danco - Apr. 18, 1972 (vault).

Capt. J. W. Young - died Oct. 18, 1888, age 54 yrs., Signal Corps. CSA.

LOT 288
Ave. 5, Old 100
Owner - Norman Cassell
Edward Ward Martin - July 8, 1974.
Virginia Martin - Jan. 7, 1951, age 60 yrs.
William Hozzard Wigg Cassell - Sept. 9, 1972 (vault).
Virginia Stevens Cassell - 1859-1923, age 63 yrs.
Norman Cassell - May 3, 1948, age 89 yrs.

LOT 289
Ave. 4, Old 91
Owners - George and Robert Barrett
Robert H. Barrett - buried Apr. 3, 1889, age 1 yr. 4 mos.
R. H. Barrett - stillborn, buried May 27, 1886.
Robert Harwood Barrett - 1887-1889, age 1 yr.
Annie Brown Barrett - 1851-1889, age 28 yrs.
Annie Hall Barrett - 1862-1890, age 27 yrs.
Mary Hall Barrett - 1885-1903, age 18 yrs.
Dona P. Barrett - 1858-1924, age 66 yrs.
George H. Barrett - 1845-1908, age 63 yrs.
Charles Barrett - Oct. 17, 1946 (cremated).
Dana Barrett - Nov. 30, 1882, age 2 yrs. 6 mos.
Ethel Wharton Barrett - 1888-1897, age 8 yrs.
Mary G. Barrett - June 28, 1895, age 7 mos.
Robert Barrett - stillborn, Jan. 20, 1896.
George H. Barrett - Aug. 29, 1884, age 1 day.

LOT 290
Ave. 5, Old 999
Owner - C. A. Ironmonger
3 graves - no names.

LOT 291
Ave. 4, Old 90
Owners - John King and P. C. Trugien
Mary E. Walton - buried July 16, 1885, age 4 mos.
Lot filled, no other interment c/o Paul C. Trugien.
No names listed.

LOT 292
Ave. 4, Old 88
Owner - Charles Cassell

Eveleen Cassell - 1860-1890, age 29 yrs.
Jane Cassell - 1831-1915, age 83 yrs.
Miss Ella J. Cassell - Mar. 25, 1938, age 84 yrs.
Virginius O. Cassell - 1826-1891, age 64 yrs., Capt. 61st Va. Inf.
   CSA.
Sarah Cassell - 1805-1867, age 61 yrs.
Charles Cassell - 1793-1855, age 61 yrs.
Charles M. Cassell - 1857-1923, age 67 yrs.

LOT 292
Ave. 5, Old 98
Owner - Methodist Church
Note: Some of these bodies moved from Old Methodist Church
   Cemetery located at site of Old Monumental Methodist
   Church Yard in Portsmouth. Some of the bodies are still
   located at the site of the old cemetery.
William Porter - buried May 3, 1927.
William Bloxom - buried Apr. 25, 1927.
Mrs. William Bloxom - buried Apr. 25, 1927.
Mrs. Mary Bell - died Nov. 27, 1820, age 21 yrs.
Francis A. Bloxom - died Nov. 29, 1836, age 35 yrs.
Mary Fisher - 1815-1879, age 63 yrs.
Rev. James L. Fisher - 1813-1882.
Rev. Daniel Hall, M.D. - died Oct. 19, 1841, age 73 yrs.
Eveline S. Spooner - died July 31, 1832, age 26 yrs.
Benjamin P. Rudd - 1791-1821, age 30 yrs.
Mary Ann Granbery - died Aug. 16, 1832, age 21 yrs.
Miss Eliza Spencer - died June 22, 1831, age 24 yrs.
Ella P. Ripley - died Dec. 8, 1932, age 74 yrs.
Sarah Delaney - died July 10, 1912, age 70 yrs.
Fanny Carter - died Mar. 10, 1909, age 90 yrs.
George R. Weaver - buried May 3, 1927, age 15 yrs.
Note: Believed all 1927 dates were moved from old cemetery on
   Glasgow St.

LOT 293
Ave. 4, Old 89
Owners - Isaac Rose. Later - Frank Stanley Cooke
Mary Cooke Cassell - Apr. 7, 1944, age 83 yrs.
V. O. Cassell, Jr. - Nov. 18, 1934, age 82 yrs.
Virginia C. Cooke - Nov. 19, 1951, age 61 yrs.
Frank S. Cooke - Sept. 25, 1950, age 68 yrs.
Sarah Smith Cooke Rose - 1805-1892, age 87 yrs.
Isaac Rose - Jan. 25, 1867, age 65 yrs.

LOT 294
Ave. 5, Old 97
Owners - Cocke and Ivy
Alice G. Stiles - June 20, 1902, age 5 mos.
Harry Cocke Stiles - Oct. 22, 1906, age 2 mos.
Mary G. H. Ross - buried Nov. 18, 1901, age 8 days.
Clinton E. Stiles - buried Aug. 24, 1899, age 5 hrs.
J. B. Drewry - CSA.
Rebecca A. Smith - 1835-1857, age 21 yrs.
Isaac Odeon - May 22, 1839, age 30 yrs.
Nettie Ina Cocke - 1844-1902, age 5 yrs.
Isaac Ann Odeon - Nov. 3, 1842, age 3 yrs. 2 mos.
Willie Ivy Smith - 1856-1857, age 2 yrs.
William Gaston Cocke - 1845-1911, age 65 yrs.

LOT 295
Ave. 4, Old 88
Owner - Charles Cassell
Eveleen Cassell - 1860-1890, age 29 yrs.
Jane Cassell - 1831-1915, age 83 yrs.
Virginius O. Cassell - 1826-1891, age 64 yrs., Capt. 61st Va. Inf.
   CSA.
Sarah Cassell - 1805-1867, age 61 yrs.
Charles Cassell - 1793-1855, age 61 yrs.
Miss Ella J. Cassell - died Mar. 25, 1938, age 84 yrs.
Charles M. Cassell - 1857-1923, age 67 yrs.

LOT 296
Ave. 5, Old 96
Owner - Herman Mathews
Wiley B. Mathews - Aug. 24, 1943, age 53 yrs.
Wilmont J. Rodgers - Aug. 26, 1945, age 64 yrs.
Annie M. Rodgers - Sept 20, 1952, age 72 yrs.
John Wilmot Rodgers - Aug. 26, 1922, age 14 yrs.
Caroline M. Mathews - Aug. 19, 1960, age 78 yrs.
Christopher C. Mathews - 1851-1928, age 77 yrs.
Lizzie H. Mathews - 1856-1927, age 71 yrs.
Herman Mathews - 1812-1886, age 73 yrs.
Sarah L. Mathews - Apr. 27, 1906, age 91 yrs.
James H. Mathews - Oct. 28, 1884, age 31 yrs.

LOT 297
Ave. 4, Old 87
Owner - Benjamin Spratley
Benjamin Spratley - died Sept. 10, 1856, War 1812.

Joanna Schutte Spratley - 1795-1879.
Mary Louisa Guthrie - Feb. 16, 1917, age 68 yrs.
Annette Caroline Guthrie - Nov. 10, 1923, age 72 yrs.
Jeanne Agnes Guthrie - Nov. 18, 1910, age 49 yrs.
B. C. Spratley, M.D. - 1819-1865, age 46 yrs.
Monument
John Julius Guthrie, Jr. - died Dec. 3, 1903, age 59 yrs., Midshipman CSN.
Benjamin Wilburne Guthrie - 1841-1895, Lt. CSN.
Willie Conrad Guthrie - July 6, 1875.
Capt. John Julius Guthrie - 1815-1877, CSN.
Louisa A. Spratley Guthrie - 1821-1900, age 78 yrs.
Note: Dec. 2, 1840 - USN John Julius Guthrie married Louisa
Sarah Spratley, eldest daughter of Benjamin Spratley,
married by Rev. Moriarty.
Apr. 30, 1818 - Benjamin Spratley married Johanna
Schulte, surety - Richard Webb.
Beacon Newspaper - Jan. 25 - Married Thursday, Alfred
M. Wilson to Miss Joanna Olivia Spratley, youngest daughter
of Benjamin Spratley.

LOT 298
Ave. 5, Old 95
Owner - Leonard Cocke
Charles L. Cocke - Aug. 4, 1854, age 51 yrs.
Ann R. Cocke - Aug. 5, 1855, age 53 yrs.
Buller Cocke - 1777-1838.
Nathaniel Cocke - Feb. 4, 1837, age 50 yrs.
Theodosia C. Cocke Bilisoly - 1828-1849 yrs.
Florence Coles - buried Aug. 29, 1893, age 25 yrs.

LOT 299
Ave. 4, Old 86
Owners - John Cocke and Martha M. Clarke, Certificate 232
Kate M. Cocke - Oct. 7, 1912, age 75 yrs.
John Nathaniel Cocke - 1835-1892, age 57 yrs., CSA.
Catherine V. Cocke - Dec. 24, 1861, age 5 days (vault).
W. H. Cocke - Surgeon 14th Va. Inf. CSA.
Irving C. Jernigan - June 16, 1987 (cremains).
Ida C. Cocke - June 24, 1872, age 44 yrs.
Nancy Cocke - Feb. 25, 1868, age 72 yrs.
Brick grave - no name.
Louisiana Hayden - died July 18, 1843, age 23 yrs. 6 mos.
William Henry Cocke - Mar. 6, 1823, age 32 yrs., Lt. USN.

LOT 300
Ave. 5, Old 94
Owner - W. B. Davis
Virginess Haynes - buried Mar. 22, 1893.
Lt. V. Haynes - 61st Va. Inf. CSA.
J. K. Haynes - 16th Va. Inf. CSA.
E. A. Davis - buried Dec. 19, 1895, age 84 yrs.

LOT 301
Ave. 4, Old 85
Owners - Chambers and White
Sarah A. Chambers - Jan. 3, 1833.
George W. Chambers - 1831-1855, age 24 yrs. (yellow fever).
Caroline A. Chambers - died Sept. 28, 1852.
James Chambers - Aug. 12, 1832.
Mrs. C. H. Lynch - Feb. 10, 1918, age 67 yrs.
Sarah H. White - May 13, 1852, age 62 yrs.
Argyra H. W. Lynch - 1849-1918, age 68 yrs.
John L. Lynch - 1847-1926, age 78 yrs.
Note: Capt. George Chambers, native of Northern State, citizen
many years of Portsmouth. Member Common Council, placed
on Sanitary Committee superintending the transportation of
the sick to the hospital during the yellow fever epidemic of
1855. While employed in this position became victim, and
after few days of severe illness, he died Aug. 21, 1855. He
was head of the Fire Dept., Superintendent of Norfolk County
Ferry. About one year before his death, was member of Odd
Fellows, Commissioner of Public Schools, and director in
Savings Bank, Sept. 20, 1830. Capt. George Chambers mar
ried Caroline White, surety - J. W. Murdaugh. Caroline
White Chambers died in 1852 of attack of yellow fever; son,
George W. Chambers, born 1831, died late Aug. 1855, also of
yellow fever; husband, Capt. George Chambers died Aug. 21,
1855; one child survived.

LOT 302
Ave. 5, Old 93
Owner - Dr. Micks
Ann B. Micks - died July 21, 1891, age 85 yrs.
Wentworth B. Micks - Oct. 30, 1864, age 62 yrs.
Margaret Micks - July 21, 1862, age 83 yrs.
Ann Wentworth Hannah - May 6, 1842, age 65 yrs.

LOT 303
Ave. 4, Old 84

Owners - Collins and Jones
William Jones Williams - Aug. 10, 1924, age 63 yrs.
Henry Bascom Jones - 1839-1855, age 16 yrs.
William A. Jones - age 7 mos.
Virginia Luke - 1837-1868, age 31 yrs.
John Wesley Luke - 1828-1866, age 38 yrs.
Martha Ann Jones - Sept. 25, 1842, age 18 yrs.
Mary Jones - 1801-1875, age 73 yrs.
William Jones - 1793-1855, age 62 yrs.
Elizabeth Collins - Mar. 8, 1832, age 60 yrs.
Mary E. Williams - Apr. 1, 1906, age 75 yrs.
Margaret Lee Williams - Dec. 3, 1931, age 68 yrs.
William A. Jones - age 7 mos.

LOT 304
Ave. 5, Old 92
Owner - William White, N/H
Surgeon L. White - CSA.
William White - June 26, 1878, age 78 yrs.
Dr. William A. White - Jan. 10, 1868, age 37 yrs.
Mary Franklin Philpotts - June 28, 1936, age 8 yrs.
Louisa Cotton Mausi - stillborn, Jan. 18, 1905.
Mausi - infant, Oct. 14, 1900.
Robert Burgess Mann - Aug. 3, 1898, age 11 mos.
Mann - infant, buried Oct. 14, 1900.

LOT 305
Ave. 4, Old 83
Owners - B. O'Niel and J. A. Milligan
Jane R. Milligan - buried Apr. 11, 1889, age 70 yrs.
Nellie Milligan - Nov. 12, 1920, age 65 yrs.
5 graves - no name.

LOT 306
Ave. 5, Old 92
Owner - James Brown, Sr., S/H
Henry Clay Brown - May 4, 1908, age 64 yrs.
James Brown - child, Sept. 25, 1884.
James Brown - Oct. 26, 1903, age 97 yrs.
J. B. Brown - Engr. CSN.
Ann Brown - Mar. 15, 1842, age 31 yrs.
H. Brown - CSA.

LOT 307
Ave. 5, Old 56

Owner - C. W. Murdaugh, Jr.
Claudius Walke Murdaugh, III - March 21, 1975 (vault).
Ann Murdaugh - Apr. 6, 1942, age 77 yrs.
Claudius Walke Murdaugh, Jr. - June 26, 1907, age 45 yrs.
Miss Esther Wilson Murdaugh - Aug. 18, 1938, age 18 yrs.
Nannie Bayton Wyatt Murdaugh - July 24, 1933, age 31 yrs.
James Arthur Murdaugh - Dec. 12, 1962.
Venetta Fredricka Wyatt Murdaugh - Aug. 30, 1982 (vault).
Claudius Wilson Murdaugh - June 2, 1891, age 2 yrs.
Mary Murdaugh - July 29, 1898, age 1 yr. 3 mos.
Weaver - stillborn, Dec. 15, 1919.

LOT 308
Ave. 6, Old 57
Owner - R. J. Armistead
Griswald - stillborn, June 23, 1913.
Ann E. Scott - buried Nov. 3, 1886, age 65 yrs.
Susan H. Griswald - Mar. 17, 1948, age 55 yrs.
Robert J. Armistead - Mar. 10, 1911, age 55 yrs.
Mary Louise Hodges Armistead - Dec. 14, 1927, age 67 yrs.
Mary A. Griswald Hodges - 1829-1916, age 87 yrs.
W. H. Armistead - Oct. 17, 1951, age 65 yrs.
Elizabeth Parson - May 4, 1945, age 24 yrs.
Robert J. Armistead - Oct. 15, 1956, age 59 yrs.

LOT 309
Ave. 5, Old 55
*Owners - Ironmonger, Mrs. Lena M. Hodges and Mrs. Annie
   Williams, S/H*
Joan Taylor - Dec. 24, 1908, age 51 yrs.
Sarah E. Spring - July 4, 1919, age 58 yrs.
James W. Spring - Apr. 10, 1899, age 34 yrs.
Robert B. Taylor - Dec. 4, 1910, age 65 yrs.
John W. Taylor - Apr. 15, 1915, age 63 yrs.
James A. Spring - Oct. 19, 1900, age 34 yrs.
Robert Lee Williams - Apr. 6, 1982 (cremated).
Annie F. Williams - Jan. 4, 1965.
Harvey Edward Williams - Sept. 22, 1956, age 81 yrs.

LOT 310
Ave. 6, Old 58
Owner - Henry Flemming (ten-grave plot)
Henry Flemming - Jan. 27, 1898, age 65 yrs.
Mary Jane Wallace - Dec. 11, 1920, age 58 yrs.
Laura Culpepper - Dec. 4, 1951, age 82 yrs.

James Frederick Culpepper - June 13, 1936, age 76 yrs.
J. T. Flemming - Apr. 16, 1908, age 52 yrs.
William H. Flemming - Jan. 6, 1892, age 29 yrs.
Sarah Flemming - Mar. 29, 1886, age 53 yrs.
Sarah Culpepper - Apr. 27, 1984 (vault).
Bettie Flemming - Oct. 5, 1889, age 32 yrs.

LOT 311
Ave. 5, Old 54
Owners - Jessie M. Overton and Robert A. Hutchins
H. W. White - buried Mar. 19, 1898, age 1 yr.
Ruth L. Hutchins - Aug. 27, 1915, age 2 yrs. 6 mos.
Laura H. Overton - May 22, 1956, age 75 yrs.
Jessie Overton - May 1, 1951, age 73 yrs.
Robert A. Hutchins - Nov. 6, 1910, age 72 yrs.
Mary Ellen Barrett Hutchins - Apr. 10, 1908, age 65 yrs.
E. Linwood Hutchins - Mar. 5, 1896, age 20 yrs.

LOT 312
Ave. 6, Old 59
Owner - Mrs. W. A. Mathieson, N/H
Archabald Mathieson - Aug. 13, 1888, age 68 yrs.
Annie B. Vaughan - Apr. 19, 1895, age 33 yrs.
Mathieson - stillborn, Oct. 6, 1893.
William A. Mathieson - Nov. 26, 1907, age 57 yrs.
Thursa Herbert Mathieson - Mar. 27, 1922, age 66 yrs.

LOT 313
Ave. 5, Old 53
Owner - Susan Sadler Peters, N/H
Jane Little Peters - Aug. 21, 1969 (vault).
William Henry Peters - Nov. 24, 1957, age 84 yrs.
James H. Peters, Jr. - age 67 yrs.
Mary A. R. Peters - 1880-1902, age 22 yrs.
James H. Peters - 1839-1890, age 51 yrs., CSA.
Susan Sadler Peters - 1845-1926, age 81 yrs.
Sue Peters - 1874-1881, age 7 yrs.
Edward W. Peters - 1883-1885, age 2 yrs.
Minor Julius Peters - 1881-1923, age 42 yrs.
Sadler Peters - 1872-1888, age 16 yrs.

LOT 314
Ave. 6, Old 59
Owner - J. S. Rogers
V. F. Stokes - June 5, 1935, age 84 yrs.

Annie L. Stokes - Dec. 2, 1914, age 51 yrs.
Josephine E. Stokes - Aug. 25, 1938, age 76 yrs.
James S. Rogers - Sept. 26, 1921, age 75 yrs.
Emily Missouri Rogers - Mar. 17, 1939, age 90 yrs.

LOT 315
Ave. 5, Old 53
Owner - L. Stringer, S/H
Robert H. Stringer - June 13, 1901, age 10 yrs. 9 mos.
Hunter L. Stringer - buried July 13, 1888, age 3 yrs. 1 mo.
John Russell - buried June 24, 1892, age 64 yrs. 5 mos.
Stringer - child, buried Aug. 19, 1895, age 6 days.
Stringer - stillborn, Dec. 16, 1896.
Catherine I. Stringer - Feb. 17, 1903, age 42 yrs.
Hurbert R. Stringer - Sept. 30, 1899, age 13 yrs.

LOT 316
Ave. 6, Old 60
Owner - T. C. Virnelson
Elizabeth Virnelson Ferebee - Nov. 10, 1909 age 32 yrs.
Jeanette Roper Ferebee - June 13, 1911, age 6 yrs.
Joseph Ferebee - Oct. 27, 1941, age 75 yrs.
Leon H. Virnelson - Nov. 25, 1947, age 77 yrs.
Mrs. Leon Virnelson
Dorothy L. Ferebee - June 1904, age 1 yr.
Harriett Herbert Virnelson - May 19, 1901, age 65 yrs.
Thomas B. Virnelson - Oct. 31, 1906, age 72 yrs., CSA.
Claude Virnelson - Apr. 20, 1952, age 90 yrs.
Mary Susan Griffith Virnelson - 1845-1925, age 79 yrs.
Clearwood Virnelson - Mar. 25, 1938, age 79 yrs.
Jesse L. Faison, Jr. - Mar. 26, 1898, age 18 yrs.
Marion Herbert Virnelson - 1893-1938 (cremated).

LOT 317
Ave. 5, Old 52
Owner - Margaret Ainsworth
Elizabeth Wall - 1841-1917, age 57 yrs.
Margaret Ainsworth - 1831-1916, age 85 yrs.
Andrew Ainsworth - 1829-1888, age 56 yrs.
Mary W. Hughes - 1810-1875, age 65 yrs. or 1800-1875, age 75
    yrs. ?
Robert W. Hughes - 1850-1903, age 52 yrs.
Daniel J. Ainsworth - 1860-1908, age 47 yrs.
Annie M. Ainsworth - 1870-1916, age 46 yrs.
Clara A. Ainsworth - 1856-1937, age 82 yrs.

LOT 318
Ave. 6, Old 61
Owner - R. E. Glassett
Robert Glassett - died Apr. 15, 1922, age 52 yrs.
Virginia A. Glassett - died May 23, 1908, age 60 yrs.
Blanche Glassett - buried June 12, 1888, age 16 yrs.
Robert Emmett Glassett - died Oct. 20, 1898, age 57 yrs.
Mary S. Glassett - died Dec. 12, 1948, age 74 yrs.
M. A. Glassett - buried May 7, 1889, age 53 yrs.
Frederick Glassett - died Jan. 27, 1950, age 72 yrs.

LOT 319
Ave. 5, Old 51
Owner - Dr. J. S. Hope, N/H
Leslie C. Hall - Dec. 3, 1913, age 51 yrs.
Flo Caston Hall - Feb. 2, 1950, age 78 yrs.
Dr. J. Shirley Hope, N.S.N - June 30, 1896, age 28 yrs.
Nicholson - stillborn.
Virginia Lee Roper - Aug. 6, 1889, age 24 yrs.

LOT 320
Ave. 6, Old 62
Owner - Dr. F. S. Hope
Stanley Hope - died June 13, 1887, age 7 mos.
John Meredith Hope - Sept. 2, 1888, age 3 mos.
Shirley Hope - Aug. 28, 1893, age 9 mos.
Gilman - stillborn, July 10 1924.
William Meredith Hope - 1811-1897, age 86 yrs., CSA.
Virginia Frances Hope - 1830-1902, age 72 yrs.
Dr. Frank Hope - Sept. 26, 1927, age 71 yrs.
Annie W. Hope - Jan. 19, 1944, age 79 yrs.
Mary Hope Brodrick - Feb. 19, 1955, age 65 yrs.

LOT 321
Ave. 5, Old 51
Owner - Charles B. Fletcher, S/H
Walter S. Fletcher - age 4 mos.
George T. Simpson - age 14 days.
Linwood H. Wilder - age 4 mos.
William Hope Roper - May 15, 1888, age 4 mos.
Lillie Fletcher - age 3 mos.
Bettie E. Fletcher - Feb. 28, 1896, age 29 yrs.
Charles B. Fletcher - Aug. 26, 1924, age 69 yrs.
Ella Bell Fletcher - Jan. 23, 1952, age 81 yrs.

LOT 322
Ave. 6, Old 63
Owner - Mrs. George Roberts
George T. Roberts - Dec. 1, 1947, age 86 yrs.
George S. Roberts - Sept. 21, 1883, age 49 yrs.
Mary E. Roberts - Feb. 22, 1914, age 74 yrs.
Ada L. Roberts - Aug. 1, 1889, age 11 yrs. 8 mos.
Effie Roberts - Nov. 9, 1892, age 6 1/2 mos.
Ann Roberts - Feb. 12, 1898, age 53 yrs.

LOT 323
Ave. 5, Old 50
Owners - Elizabeth Hickman, S/H - Transferred to Rufus J. Old, June 19, 1963.
Fred Hill, May 21, 1974.
Edward T. Hickman, Sr. - Mar. 8, 1883, age 41 yrs.
Elizabeth Hickman - June 4, 1896, age 60 yrs.
Edward T. Hickman, Jr. - Sept. 11, 1931, age 60 yrs.

LOT 324
Ave. 6, Old 154
Owner - Col. Mordecai Cooke
Col. Mordecai Cooke - 1785-1845.
Capt. John K. Cooke - 1812-1887, age 75 yrs., CSA.
Mrs. Fanny B. Cooke - 1818-1867.
Henry Beauregard Cooke - 1861-1861.
Ella Mason Cooke Chandler - 1841-1906, age 63 yrs.
Margaret A. Cooke White - 1839-1920, age 81 yrs.
Mrs. M. F. Cooke - 1840-1894, age 53 yrs.

LOT 325
Ave. 5, Old 159
Owner - M. Cooke
Edward Lee Ross - July 17, 1897, age 1 yr. 7 mos.
Harvey Eagan Ross - May 9, 1899, age 2 mos.
E. Florence Kennedy Cooke - 1893-1912, age 18 yrs.
Thomas Paul Cooke - 1854-1915.
Minnie F. Cooke - Apr. 19, 1948, age 75 yrs.
J. Carroll Cooke - 1856-1925, age 56 yrs.
Virginia Cooke - July 17, 1942, age 94 yrs.
Olivia S. Cooke - 1823-1911, age 88 yrs.
P. H. Cooke - 1818-1872.

LOT 326
Ave. 6, Old 153
Owner - Col. George Blow
Col. George Blow - 1787-1870.
Eliza Waller Blow - 1791-1841.
Richard Blow - Feb. 3, 1833, age 87 yrs.
Mrs. Frances Blow - 1767-1838, age 71 yrs.
Mrs. Mary M. Warren - Nov. 30, 1852, age 76 yrs.
Emma Blow Blacknall - Dec. 31, 1897, age 85 yrs.
Dr. George Blacknall - Jan. 20, 1862, Surgeon CSN.
Fanny Blow Blacknall - 1842-1934, age 85 yrs.

LOT 327
Ave. 5, Old 158
Owner - George Blow - Graves transferred to John Paul C.
Hanbury and Jean C. Hanbury on Aug. 31, 1981.

LOT 328
Ave. 6, Old 152
Owner - Jethro Jenkins
Eliza O. Scott - June 1, 1899, age 77 yrs.
Jethro A. Jenkins - Feb. 4, 1869, age 65 yrs.
Jennet L. Jenkins - Sept. 8, 1845, age 34 yrs.
Adj. J. S. Jenkins - died July 3, 1863, age 31 yrs., 14th Va. Inf.
    CSA.
Virginia F. Jenkins - Sept. 8, 1849, age 18 yrs.
Indiana Cox Jenkins - Aug. 12, 1841, age 6 yrs.
A. R. Foster - Signal Corp. CSA.
A. T. Foster, M.D. - Nov. 11, 1858, age 43 yrs.
Missouri Asbury Jenkins - 1838-1854.
William Benthall Jenkins - Nov. 15, 1856, age 5 yrs.
Louisiana E. Jenkins - Aug. 12, 1841, age 13 mos.
Eliza C. Foster - buried Sept. 4, 1895, age 78 yrs.
Note: Eliza Sullen born Williamsburg, Va., wife of Archibald T.
    Foster whose parents were Archibald T. Foster and Frances
    Tallman, died Feb. 19, 1841, information from letter file in
    Portsmouth Library from John A. Foster, 11 Sunrise St.,
    Plainview, New York 11803 in 1989.

LOT 329
Ave. 5, Old 158
Owner - George Blow
Note: Perpetual care paid by check, United Bank, Nov. 6, 1970,
    recorded Nov. 10, 1970. Aug. 13, 1981, Graves 1, 2, 3, 4, 9,
    and 10, via City Clerk, transferred to John Paul C. Hanbury

and Jean C. Hanbury.
Graves on this lot :
Lucy Blacknall - Feb. 12, 1942, age 88 yrs.
Emma Blacknall - born 1846, died Dec. 18, 1911, age 65 yrs.

LOT 330
Ave. 5, Old 157
Owner - William Emmerson
Charles Bilisoly - June 30, 1884, age 3 yrs.
E. P. Emmerson - Apr. 25, 1885, age 4 yrs.
Fannie Diggs Emmerson - 1846-1914, age 67 yrs.
William Emmerson - 1843-1918, age 75 yrs. Co. C, 16th Va.
 Regt. CSA.

LOT 331
Ave. 5, Old 157
Owners - Mrs. Ann Armistead and Lumley, S/H
Mrs. Elizabeth A. W. Cowley - Nov. 19, 1854, age 39 yrs.
Mrs. Ann Armistead - Sept. 6, 1847, age 67 yrs.
Mary Louise Lumley - Mar. 1, 1919.
J. W. Lumley - Jan. 8, 1923, age 76 yrs., Co. 1, N.C. CSA.

LOT 332
Ave. 6, Old 151
Owner - Robert M. Bain, N/H
Anna Bain - Aug. 26, 1928, age 85 yrs.
John Jacks - stillborn.
Robert M. Bain - 1816-1880, USN and CSN.
Sarah Elizabeth White Bain
Sarah W. Bain - Mar. 5, 1959, age 92 yrs.
Mary Bain Chapman - May 28, 1950, age 83 yrs.
Mary W. Bain - 1841-1913, age 72 yrs.
Note: Not noted in plot book but buried with this family is the
 name:
William Chapman - May 25, 1860-Sept. 27, 1930.

LOT 333
Ave. 5, Old 156
Owner - John Lash, N/H
Florence G. Brown - buried Aug. 20, 1889, age 31 yrs.
Stillborn of E. L. Lash - Aug. 12, 1891.
Child of E. L. Lash - buried Aug. 18, 1895, age 8 days.
Mary E. Lash - 1819-1885.
George F. Lash - 1837-1838.
Anna B. Lash - 1843-1844.

Sarah B. Lash - 1846-1847.
Florence A. Lash - 1849-1950.
Ann F. Lash - Apr. 10, 1855, age 76 yrs.
John Lash - June 10 1882, age 65 yrs.
Mary Frances Lash - Oct. 19, 1939, age 89 yrs.
James Peek Lash - Oct. 3, 1933, age 88 yrs.

LOT 334
Ave. 6, Old 151
Owner - David Bain, S/H
David A. Bain
Mrs. Anna Augusta Bain - Aug. 26, 1828.
Fanstina H. Booth Bain - Sept. 21, 1894, age 63 yrs.
William Chapman - 1860-1930 (see Chapman Lot 332), age 70
    yrs.

LOT 335
Ave. 5, Old 156
Owner - Yeates, S/H
Sarah E. Brickhouse - Jan. 30, 1907, age 31 yrs.
Brickhouse - stillborn of S. E. and A. A. Brickhouse, Jan. 29,
    1907.

LOT 336
Ave. 6, Old 61
Owner - Hanrah B. Huestis
Samuel B. Gibson - 1884-1931, age 46 yrs.
Imogene Lucille Gibson - Feb. 5, 1977 (vault).
John Robert Gibson - Mar. 30, 1983 (vault).
Hanrah B. Huestis - Sept. 23, 1843, age 42 yrs.
Oney Hall Edwards - 1827-1908, age 81 yrs., Surgeon 9th Va.
    Inf. CSA.
Elizabeth Ann Edwards - 1830-1910, age 80 yrs.
Newton Edwards - Mar. 20, 1940, age 69 yrs.
Oney H. Edwards, Jr. - 1853-1905, age 51 yrs.
Laura Edwards - Oct. 29, 1934, age 78 yrs.

LOT 337
Ave. 5, Old 155
Owner - Rev. Thomas Hume
George T. Flournoy - July 21, 1981 (vault).
Sarah Hume Flournoy - Apr. 27, 1976 (vault).
Seaborn J. Flournoy - Jan. 28, 1979.
Rev. Thomas Hume - 1812-1875.

Mary Ann Gregory Hume - Mar. 18, 1862, age 47 yrs.
Jennie Hume Clark - Nov. 16, 1866, age 25 yrs.
Jeter Hume, 1849-1850, and Elizabeth H. Hume, 1842-1844 -
    children of Thomas and Mary Hume.
Lemuel Peebles Hume - 1875-1876.
Flournoy - stillborn, July 17, 1934.
Francis Lee Threadcraft - 1871-1923, age 52 yrs.
Sarah Nash Threadcraft - Mar. 10, 1970 (vault).
Monument

LOT 338
Ave. 6, Old D1
Owner - Christine Diggs
Emily Johnson - buried Oct. 18, 1900, age 4 mos.
Diggs - stillborn, buried Sept. 6, 1890.
C. Y. Diggs - 1810-1860.
Linda Diggs - 1858-1862.
Frances H. Diggs - 1817-1901, age 84 yrs.
William Waller Diggs - 1839-1869, 16th Va. Inf. CSA.
William Waller Diggs - 1878-1885, age 6 yrs.
Carrie A. Diggs - 1847-1902, age 55 yrs.
C. C. Diggs - 1844-1918, age 74 yrs., 3rd Ga. Regt. CSA.
Henry B. Hardy - Oct. 5, 1952, age 72 yrs.
Lola D. Hardy - Feb. 10, 1956, age 82 yrs.
Emma J. Higgins - 1837-1902, age 65 yrs.
Charles W. Higgins - 1838-1902, age 63 yrs.

LOT 339
Ave. 5, Old 190
Owner - John Jack
Eugenius Alexander Jack - 1840-1911, age 71 yrs., Engr. CSN.
Mary Redman Jack - 1858-1925, age 67 yrs.
Mary E. D. Jack - July 8, 1957, age 80 yrs.
Laurence McKay Jack - Dec. 24, 1955, age 85 yrs.
John Jack - 1819-1902, age 82 yrs., CSA.
Mary Lizzie Jack - 1848-1911, age 63 yrs.
John L. Jack - 1850-1912, age 61 yrs.
Bettie Jack - May 21, 1943, age 87 yrs.
William Roland Bruce - buried Jan. 11, 1971 (vault).

LOT 340
Ave. 6, Old 189
Owner - Eastwood
Powers - stillborn, buried June 5, 1909.
Mary Helen Powers Hatchett - 1899-1926, age 26 yrs.

Virginius Powers - Oct. 1, 1933, age 79 yrs.
Mrs. Mary Eastwood Powers - Aug. 21, 1938, age 82 yrs.
Charles Eastwood - Feb. 24, 1944, age 80 yrs.
Columbia Eastwood - Aug. 18, 1950, age 91 yrs.
Edward W. Eastwood - Sept. 26, 1883, age 52 yrs.
Sarah A. Eastwood - Jan. 23, 1908, age 83 yrs.
Jane Winslow Powers - died May 30, 1917, age 7 mos.

LOT 341
Ave. 5, Old Y
Owner - John Roby
Susanna B. Roby - 1837-1853, age 17 yrs.
Elenor Ann Roby - Apr. 25, 1887, age 78 yrs.
John T. Roby - Feb. 18, 1887, age 54 yrs.

LOT 342
Ave. 6, Old A1
Owner - Robert C. Rodman
Lillian Camillia Savage - Oct. 13, 1930, age 61 yrs.
Hughlett A. Savage - buried Aug. 11, 1891, age 2 1/2 yrs.
R. E. Wilson - Feb. 14, 1902, age 38 yrs.
Willis B. Dail - Aug. 19, 1856, age 33 yrs.
Virginia A. Dail - Nov. 16, 1867, age 36 yrs.
Robert C. Rodman - Sept. 19, 1855, age 53 (yellow fever), USN.
Sarah Rodman - Sept. 7, 1872, age 67.
Nola Wininger - July 8, 1942, age 79 yrs.
Mary C. Rodman - 1850-1900, age 52 yrs.
Grave marked J. W. E.
Guyton D. Savage - Jan. 17, 1941, age 74 yrs.

LOT 343
Old X
Owner - Dr. T. H. Bagwell, N/H
T. H. Bagwell - buried Sept. 17, 1895, age 33 yrs.
Annie D. Grubbs - died Sept. 15, 1917, age 54 yrs.
Imogene Bagwell - died Mar. 5, 1900, age 69 yrs.
Dr. Thomas H. Bagwell - died Apr. 8, 1888, age 67 yrs.

LOT 344
Ave. 5, Old X
Owner - Capt. John R. White, S/H
Mary Weston White - Mar. 1, 1932, age 77 yrs.
Frederick Burns Hill - Sept. 27, 1963.
Mary White Hill - May 24, 1974 (vault).
Imogene Montague - Nov. 22, 1955, age 92 yrs.

Thomas J. Montague - 1823-1898, age 77 yrs.
Imogene Weston White - 1829-1910, age 81 yrs.
Capt. John R. White - 1826-1897, Co. A, 3rd Va. Inf. CSA Picketts Div.

LOT 345
Ave. 5, Old W2
Owner - Alice Adams, N/H
L. N. Moreland - Jan. 17, 1896, age 20 yrs.
Woodson H. Moore - Apr. 24, 1934, age 59 yrs.
Logan Thomas Adams - 1870-1902.

LOT 346
Ave. 6, Old 229
Owner - E. W. Tabb, N/H
Annie Trugien Gaskins - 1874-1925, age 50 yrs.
Annie Grace Tabb - 1852-1922, age 70 yrs.
Edward Watts Tabb - 1848-1916, age 68 yrs.

LOT 347
Ave. 5, Old W2
Owners - William Hutson, S/H - Bought by William Hodges and Laurence S. Baker, 1951.
Mary Hall - July 27, 1913, age 76 yrs.
Martha E. Schroader - Feb. 7, 1916, age 45 yrs.
Herbert M. Schroader - June 25, 1904, age 2 mos.
Julia M. Schroader - June 19, 1902, age 11 days.
Laurence Baker - Nov. 27, 1955, age 68 yrs.
William Hutson - July 30, 1907, age 44 yrs., USN.
Elsie J. Baker - May 11, 1974 (vault).
William H. Baker - Aug. 8, 1953, age 68 yrs.

LOT 348
Ave. 6, Old 229
Owner - James E. Curlin, S/H
Sallie B. Curlin - Nov. 11, 1936, age 83 yrs.
Charles Curlin - Feb. 20, 1960, age 83 yrs.
Emily W. Curlin - May 9, 1953, age 76 yrs.
James E. Curlin - 1851-1924, age 73 yrs.

LOT 349
Ave. 5, Old W1
Owners - W. H. Staples, N/H - A. O. Curling, East 1/4 of N/H
Sarah Morris - Jan. 14, 1929, age 71 yrs.
Willis N. Neville - July 7, 1889, age 2 mos.

Willie Earl Staples - Dec. 29, 1891, age 2 yrs. 2 1/2 mos.
Virginia F. Curling - Sept. 10, 1959, age 82 yrs.
Alonzo Curling - Sept. 18, 1945, age 73 yrs.

LOT 350
Ave. 6, Old 230
Owner - Wilder, N/H
William B. Wilder - July 8, 1918, age 68 yrs.
Martha B. Wilder - Dec. 17, 1903, age 67 yrs.
Ella J. Wilder - Aug. 1, 1927, age 72 yrs.
Charles C. Wilder - Oct. 7, 1943, age 81 yrs.

LOT 351
Ave. 5, Old W1
Owner - Benjamin W. Palmer, S/H
B. W. Palmer, Jr. - buried Apr. 29, 1885, age 5 yrs.
Catherine M. Palmer - buried Sept. 8, 1895, age 41 yrs.
Ben Alexander Palmer - died Apr. 15, 1885, age 31.

LOT 352
Ave. 6, Old 230
Owner - Robert P. Neville, S/H
Thomas R. Stratton - Dec. 2, 1902, age 3 mos.
Robert Hayes Neville - 1872-1931, age 59 yrs., Lt. USN.
Jesse Pearson Neville - 1869-1902, age 33 yrs.
Mollie Dines Neville - 1845-1920, age 74 yrs.
Robert Pullen Neville - 1846-1913 age 66 yrs.
Robert Hayes Neville - 1902-1902.
Jesse Overaker Neville - 1906-1935, age 27 yrs.

LOT 353
Ave. 5, Old W
Owner - Washington B. Allmond, N/H
Ethel May Allmond - Oct. 30, 1893, age 4 mos.
Thomas Williams - died May 10, 1913, age 61 yrs.
Catherine Allmond - buried Dec. 5, 1885, age 63 yrs.
Ida Virginia Allmond - buried Oct. 7, 1886, age 19 yrs.
Annie Allen Allmond - 1861-1913.
Washington Bartlett Allmond - 1862-1915.
George W. Williams - 1853-1906.

LOT 354
Ave. 6, Old Z
Owner - Stephen C. Myers
George Stephen Miller - Mar. 11, 1837, age 83 yrs.

Annetta Nash Miller Morse - 1888-1928, age 40 yrs.
Christopher Stoakes Morse - 1884-1936, age 51 yrs.
Charlie Leon Myers - 1872-1882, age 17 yrs.
Stephen C. Myers - 1872-1889, died age 59 yrs., Sergt. 9th Va.
   Inf. CSA.
Mary A. Myers - 1836-1900, age 63 yrs.
George E. Parker - 1870-1895, age 24 yrs.
Mary Miller - Oct. 10, 1941, age 86 yrs.

LOT 355
Ave. 5, Old W
Owner - Washington B. Allmond, S/H
Heston F. Brown - Apr. 23, 1932, age 78 yrs.
E. E. Hill - Mar. 4, 1903, age 11 mos.
G. L. Hill - Jan. 17, 1901, age 3 mos.
C. E. Borum - buried Dec. 13, 1897, age 60 yrs.
Marion Whitehead - buried Aug. 16, 1887, age 31 yrs.
E. G. Borum - CSA.

LOT 356
Ave. 6, Old 191
Owner - John Lash
Junious Richardson - Jan. 8, 1974 (vault).
Agnes Lash - Jan. 14, 1957.
Elder L. or Elmer S. Lash - Apr. 13, 1955, age 89 yrs.
Harry Eugene Lash - 1893-1909, age 16 yrs.
Jane Nolen Joyce - 1829-1908, age 79 yrs.
John H. Joyce - 1833-1905, age 72 yrs.
Hattie L. Lash - Aug. 28, 1947, age 92 yrs.
Charles B. Lash - 1859-1914, age 55 yrs.
J. W. Lash - died Oct. 4, 1903, age 63 yrs., 16th Va. Inf. CSA.

LOT 357
Ave. 5, Old V
Owner - John A. Chandler
Isaac D. Richardson - Sept. 21, 1905, age 31 yrs.
Mrs. Sarah Chandler - 1801-1876.
John Adams Chandler - 1795-1848.
Leonides Rosser - age 11 mos. 4 days.
H. F. Woodhouse, Jr. - buried Apr. 12, 1889, age 28 yrs., 5th Va.
   Inf. CSA (most likely killed during CSA war and reinterred).
George McKendree Chandler - Feb. 11, 1957, age 20 yrs. 8 mos.
Celio Dowell Webb - Jan. 11, 1936, age 5 hrs.

LOT 359
Ave. 5, Old 109
Owner - Edward Trugien
Ann G. T. Thomas - Sept. 9, 1855, age 33 yrs. (yellow fever).
Sarah D. Trugien - Sept. 8, 1855, age 52 yrs. (yellow fever).
Gertrude Brooks Sawyer - 1884-1937, age 51 yrs.
Francis Wharton Elliott - 1869-1923, age 54 yrs.
Walter Cooke Brooks - 1859-1931, age 70 yrs.
Mary Ferrel Trugien - 1841-1875, age 31 yrs.
Laura Frances Trugien - 1859-1907, age 47 yrs.
Gertrude Trugien Brooks - 1861-1922, age 60 yrs.
Note: Obit. Feb. 5, 1907 - Laura Frances deSales Trugien, age
   47, died yesterday morning at 3:55 A.M. in the home of her
   sister, Mrs. Walter C. Brooks, 300 Crawford St., Funeral at
   Saint Pauls Catholic, daughter of the late Edward C. and
   Mary F. Trugien.

LOT 360
Ave. 6, Old 117
Owner - Robert Emmett Crump
Note: No more burials on this lot except cremains Oct. 16, 1984.
Sarah F. Crump - Oct. 8, 1883, age 45 yrs.
George G. Joyce - Aug. 11, 1896, age 50 yrs.
Travis Grant - Sept. 17, 1839, age 32 yrs.
Lelia Lafayette Crump - Apr. 30, 1943, age 86 yrs. (vault).
William Harrison - July 17, 1859, age 79 yrs.
Johannah Harrison - July 23, 1855, age 72 yrs.
1 grave - no name.
Eugenia Schroeder - wife of Robert Emmett Crump, 1863-1933,
   age 70 yrs.
Robert Emmett Crump - 1859-1928, age 69 yrs.
David A. Crump - Aug. 3, 1876, age 47 yrs.
Fannie S. Crump - Oct. 7, 1883.
Peachy Boswell Crump - July 4, 1964 (should be on Lot 360,
   should be East end of lot at foot).
Note: Grave positioned N. and S. and curbing removed for suffi-
   cient burial space, contact Miss M. C. Watts, signed by W. H.
   Crump.

LOT 361
Ave. 5, Old 108
*Owner - Capt. John Thompson - Lola Credle purchased Graves 3
   and 4 from Winbrough and sons on Apr. 24, 1985.*
John Thompson Baird, Jr. - died July 3, 1917, age 44 yrs.
Elizabeth C. Benson - 1810-1852, age 41 yrs.

Lucrese Baird Charles - 1866-1909, age 42 yrs.
Ahrerra S. Baird - died Jan. 19, 1919, age 83 yrs.
Lt. J. Thompson Baird - died May 9, 1905, age 77 yrs., 16th Va. Inf. CSA.
Elizabeth Thompson - died June 20, 1851, age 75 yrs.
Capt. John Thompson - 1768-1847, age 78 yrs.
Maria Baird Blackstone - no data of death.
No. 4 reserved for Lola Credle.
No. 3 Byron E. Credle - Apr. 26, 1985 (vault).

LOT 362
Ave. 6, Old 116
Owner - Samuel Wilson - Sold to Louis J. Morris, Feb. 7, 1925, Deed Book 94A, Page 77.
Elizabeth Hodges - July 12, 1885, age 63 yrs.
Hickman - stillborn.
William J. Hodges - 1853-1924, age 70 yrs.
Charles A. Robinson - died May 26, 1955, age 74 yrs.
Clara Bell Robinson - died Sept. 29, 1952, age 71 yrs.
Louis J. Morris - July 1976 (vault).
Eva Pruden Morris - died Apr. 24, 1954.

LOT 363
Ave. 5, Old 107
Owner - Charles A. Grice
Henrietta W. Grice - Oct. 3, 1823.
Maria D. Grice - July 7, 1827.
Charles Robert Jordan - Nov. 14, 1813.
Emily Grice - age 10 days.
Mary Eliza Grice Jordan - 1821-1846, age 24 yrs.
Charles C. Grice - 1833-1887, age 53 yrs.
Mary E. Grice - 1838-1897, age 58 yrs.
Eliza T. Grice - Feb. 2, 1843, age 39 yrs.
Charles A. Grice - 1792-1870, age 77 yrs., War 1812.
Charles A. Grice - 1885-1885.
Susan Thoroughgood Grice - 1844-1935, age 91 yrs.
Alexander Pinkham Grice - Jan. 1, 1891, age 55 yrs.
Sam Davis - Apr. 7, 1819.
Lydia Davis - 1823
Caroline Davis - 1827.

LOT 364
Ave. 6, Old 115
Owner - Thomas Rice
Katie Mae Gerold - Nov. 26, 1923, age 1 yr. 4 mos.

Amanda Rice - Mar. 23, 1903, age 76 yrs.
John C. Baort - June 1, 1949, age 53 yrs.
William Gurney Haynes - Aug. 25, 1966 (vault).
3 graves - no names.

LOT 365
Ave. 5, Old 106
Owner - Christopher C. Stoakes
Augustus B. Stoakes - died Aug. 18, 1842.
Joice D. Stoakes - age 40 yrs.
Christopher C. Stoakes - age 71 yrs.
Susan Stoakes Knott - 1845-1907, age 62 yrs.
Ann Catherine Stoakes - Mar. 17, 1841.
Mrs. Martha A. Roser - 1814-1855.

LOT 366
Ave. 6, Old 115
Owner - Herman Matthews
1 grave - no name.
Henry J. Maddrey - 1871-1925, age 53 yrs.
Mrs. Lena Reid Maddrey - July 26, 1968, age 90 yrs. (vault).
Mary Emily Maddrey - 1908-1924, age 15 yrs.
Gilley Matthews - died May 21, 1856, age 86 yrs.

LOT 367
Ave. 5, Old 105
Owner - John C. Kaufman
Ellis M. Kaufman - June 22, 1904, age 2 yrs. 6 mos.
Alice C. Brooks - Aug. 29, 1920, age 77 yrs.
W. J. Richardson - Apr. 27, 1886, age 31 yrs.
John Carroll Kaufman - Aug. 1, 1875, age 20 days.
John C. Kaufman
B. F. Kaufman - Oct. 3, 1960, age 81 yrs.
Jeter C. Kaufman - May 1, 1951, age 74 yrs.

LOT 368
Ave. 6, Old 114
Owner - John Drewery
Miss Susie A. Drewery - Oct. 7, 1899, age 57 yrs.
Fanny Hope Drewery - Sept. 19, 1897, age 9 mos.
William E. Hawkins - May 31, 1890, age 1 yr. 11 mos.
2 graves - no names.
John B. Drewery - Aug. 22, 1900, age 61 yrs.
Annie Drewery - Oct. 15, 1899, age 7 yrs.
F. H. Drewery - June 14, 1895, age 1 yr. 1 mo.

LOT 369
Ave. 5, Old 105
Owner - Capt. Edward T. Blamire, S/H
Capt. Edward T. Blamire - died Apr. 17, 1868, age 62 yrs., 9th
    Va. Inf. CSA.
Lucretia F. Blamire - Nov. 11, 1813, age 32 yrs.
Elizabeth Blamire - Sept. 15, 1840, age 75 yrs.
Margaret Grice Blamire - Sept. 12, 1878, age 23 yrs.
Mary Elizabeth
Nathaniel Blamire - July 7, 1897, age 39 yrs.
Cornelia Frances Blamire - Nov. 12, 1883, age 58 yrs.

LOT 370
Ave. 6, Old 113
Owners - Capt. William Tee and John S. Beaton
George W. Tee - 1808-1842.
Mary A. Tee - 1810-1850.
Lizzie Veale - 1871-1885, age 13 yrs.
Sarah E. Beaton - 1835-1882.
John K. Beaton - 1833-1864, Sgt. 9th Va. Inf. CSA.
Mary A. Beaton - 1808-1891, age 82 yrs.
Mrs. Nancy Beaton - Feb. 22, 1843, age 66 yrs.
George W. Beaton - 1842-1860.
Capt. William Tee - Oct. 14, 1849, age 91 yrs.
John S. Beaton - 1802-1852.
Billie Beaton - 1840-1841.
Note: Jan. 16, 1827 - John S. Beaton married Mary Tee, daugh-
    ter of William Tee.

LOT 371
Ave. 5, Old 104
Owner - Cmdr. Alexander B. Pinkham
Mrs. Lydia H. Pinkham - 1811-1882, wife of Cmdr. A. B. Pink-
    ham.
Alexander B. Pinkham - died July 23, 1843, age 45 yrs.,
    Commander USN.
Alexna M. Kean - 1815.
Alice Farragut Kean - 1844.
Mary B. Cunninghan - Dec. 30, 1943, age 75 yrs.
Charles G. Pinkham - Apr. 6, 1865, CSA.
Raymond Cunningham - 1896-1906, age 10 yrs.
Benjamin B. Reynolds - Sept. 29, 1847, age 44 yrs.

LOT 372
Ave. 6, Old 112

Owner - Robert D. Cutherell
George A. Scott - 1854-1883.
Fannie Scott - Mar. 28, 1947, age 88 yrs.
7 graves - no names.
Mary F. Cutherell - Feb. 28, 1888, age 58 yrs.
Eva Cutherell - Nov. 1, 1885, age 21 yrs.
Mary W. Cutherell - Dec. 30, 1888, age 19 yrs.
Emily A. Williams - Dec. 17, 1889, age 23 yrs.
Emily Amelia Williams - Jan. 29, 1890, age 8 1/2 yrs.

LOT 373
Ave. 5, Old 103
Owner - Miles Washington Minter
Samuel R. Ferguson - 1821-1851.
Virginia C. Ferguson - 1827-1868.
Mary Victoria Dyson - May 15, 1891, age 57 yrs.
Emma P. Minter - 1816-1907, age 91 yrs.
Miles Washington Minter - 1809-1899, age 89 yrs.
Charles Marshall Minter - Nov. 8, 1842, age 5 yrs.
Mary Eliza Minter - Sept. 14, 1887, age 65 yrs.
Elizabeth D. Hall - Feb. 27, 1844, age 24 yrs.

LOT 374
Ave. 6, Old 111
Owner - Alfred M. Wilson
Sallie M. Wilson - 1846-1868.
Joanna O. Spratley Wilson - 1823-1900.
Alfred Mathew Wilson - 1814-1898, age 83 yrs.
Joseph Alfred Guthrie - 1900-1909, age 9 yrs.
Catherine G. Downing - Jan. 21, 1986 (vault).
Dr. Joseph A. Guthrie - was moved to Arlington County, Nov. 11, 1950.
Mary Joanna Wilson - June 11, 1811.
Henrietta S. M. Wilson - 1804-1840.
John Wilson - Sept. 26, 1843, age 67 yrs.
Sally Mathews Wilson - 1783-1870.
Mary A. B. Barron - 1802-1884, age 82 yrs.
Note: Will of Mrs. Joanna O. Wilson, dated Mar. 19, 1890, Probated Apr. 6, 1900. Estate of considerable value, distributed among her Godchildren, nieces and nephews. To the three former, $1,000.00: G. S. Vermillion, Marianna Williams, and J. J. Guthrie. The rest of her estate went to her nieces and nephews: Mary L. Guthrie, Nettie C. Guthrie, Eliza R. Ward, Jean Guthrie, John Julius Guthrie, Joseph Alfred, and B. W. Guthrie.

LOT 375, 377
Ave. 5, Old 102
Owner - James B. Potts
James A. Borum - Oct. 30, 1945, age 56 yrs.
Mary Frances Lemosy - June 26, 1853.
Mrs. Sarah Potts - Aug. 22, 1855, age 61 yrs.
James B. Potts - 1767-1839, Sailing Master USN.
James W. W. Potts - age 5 yrs.
Mary Catherine Potts - age 9 mos.
Katie Richardson - died May 3, 1887, age 6 yrs.
J. Richardson - May 2, 1894.
Betavia A. Beach - Mar. 23, 1933, age 78 yrs.

LOT 376
Ave. 6, Old 110
Owner - Brounley, N/H
Lorine Virginia Brounley - Dec. 10, 1929, age 75 yrs.
Georgana Brounley - June 10, 1910, age 71 yrs.
Rosana Brounley - July 24, 1890, age 79 yrs.
James Schooley - Sept. 26, 1908, age 73 yrs.
Elizabeth H. Brown - Mar. 18, 1889, age 74 yrs.
Clifford V. Schooley - Apr. 17, 1971 (vault).
5 graves - no names.

LOT 378
Ave. 6, Old 110
Owner - Albert G. N. Reid, S/H
Albert G. N. Reid - 1838-1864, CSA.
Catherine McGarigal - Apr. 11, 1938, age 73 yrs.
Cornelia A. Reid - 1839-1906, age 67 yrs.
Leonard Calvert Adams - May 3, 1874, age 70 yrs.
Ann Veale Adams - May 3, 1874, age 70 yrs.
Eliza Hope - 1819-1850.

LOT 379
Ave. 5, Old 101
Owner - Caleb Nash
Theodore H. Nash - Apr. 19, 1911, age 39 yrs.
John B. Horton - Feb. 24, 1961, age 88 yrs.
William C. Nash - May 25, 1837, age 5 yrs. 9 mos.
Margaret Ann Nash - Mar. 17, 1830, age 9 mos.
Ann Nash - Mar. 17, 1830, age 9 mos.
Mary F. Horton - Sept. 21, 1952, age 69 yrs.
Mary F. Nash - 1859-1929, age 69 yrs.
Meloyed Judson Nash - 1853-1902, age 43 yrs.

Mrs. Ann Lum - Sept. 20, 1842, age 65 yrs.
Mary A. Nash - 1838-1915, age 77 yrs.
George W. Nash - Oct. 5, 1940, age 66 yrs.
Sarah Nash - July 18, 1879, age 68 yrs.
Caleb Nash - 1801-1859, age 57 yrs.
David M. W. Nash - Dec. 17, 1896, age 61 yrs.

LOT 380
Ave. 7, Old 71
Owner - Henry E. Culpepper
Monument
William and Nettie Thompson - stillborn, Mar. 9, 1903.
Etta Graves - Feb. 22, 1958, age 73 yrs.
William C. Thompson - Mar. 25, 1906, age 1 yr. 10 mos.
Dr. Stanley Hope Graves - Feb. 2, 1956, age 83 yrs.
Claude E. Culpepper - May 1, 1900, age 40 yrs.
Vernon Alexander Culpepper - died Dec. 29, 1887, age 8 mos.
Maggie Hall Culpepper - Aug. 26, 1873.
Etta T. Culpepper - Mar. 28, 1933, age 70 yrs.
Dr. V. G. Culpepper - Oct. 15, 1905, age 49 yrs.
Henry E. Culpepper - Dec. 17, 1895, age 68 yrs.
Martha Helen Culpepper - Dec. 16, 1886, age 55 yrs.
Culpepper - stillborn, Apr. 17, 1888.

LOT 381
Ave. 6, Old 70
Owner - Henry E. Culpepper
Veale - stillborn of S. F. and R. Veale, buried Feb. 24, 1904.
Henry E. Culpepper, Jr. - June 10, 1899, age 46 yrs.
Medora E. Culpepper - Dec. 10, 1921, age 67 yrs.
Grant Veale - Sept. 14, 1900, age 6 days.
Ruth V. Culpepper Veale - Feb. 23, 1904, age 33 yrs.
Simeon Tee Veale - Apr. 1, 1932, age 65 yrs.
Dr. Charles Lee Culpepper - Dec. 27, 1906, age 44 yrs.
Margaret D. Allen - July 8, 1961, age 68 yrs.
Reginald B. Allen - Nov. 25, 1960, age 69 yrs.
Martha H. C. Dougan - Feb. 9, 1953, age 85 yrs.
R. E. Lee Dougan - Feb. 21, 1917, age 53 yrs.

LOT 382
Ave. 7, Old 72
Owner - Rachel Beaton
Richard P. Beaton - Sept. 7, 1907, age 54 yrs.
Annie Virginia Beaton - Feb. 21, 1928, age 73 yrs.
Rachel Beaton - June 16, 1907, age 93 yrs.

7 graves - no names.
Richard P. Beaton - July 14, 1859, age 53 yrs.
Annie E. Beaton - Aug. 28, 1886, age 37 yrs.
John L. Beaton - Nov. 11, 1907, age 57 yrs.
R. M. Beaton - Oct. 25, 1895, age 2 yrs. 10 mos.
Elise Beaton - Nov. 18, 1896, age 9 mos.
D. D. Henkel - stillborn, Jan. 27, 1892.

LOT 384
Ave. 7, Old 73
Owner - B. T. Reddick
Mary Ann Reddick - Feb. 20, 1902, age 79 yrs.
Catherine Smith - Dec. 7, 1906, age 55 yrs.
G. W. King - June 19, 1902, age 1 yr. 6 mos.
Malissa Alger - Oct. 11, 1886, age 75 yrs.
Thomas Leo Reddick - July 13, 1888, age 17 yrs.
Sarah Anne Reddick - June 3, 1921, age 74 yrs.
Burwell T. Reddick - July 16, 1922, age 72 yrs.
Burwell Reddick - June 26, 1948, age 66 yrs.

LOT 385
Ave. 6, Old 68
*Owners - W. C. Arrington, N/H - Sold to Helen N. Nash 1/5 of
    North Half, Mar. 10, 1943.*
C. Monroe Nash - June 26, 1972 (vault).
Sallie James Arrington - Apr. 4, 1887, age 32 yrs.
William C. Arrington - Nov. 5, 1894, age 44 yrs.
A. Evelyn Arrington - Jan. 26, 1916.
Sallie Arrington - Dec. 21, 1921, age 48 yrs.

LOT 386
Ave. 7, Old 74
Owner - William C. Nash, N/H
William Collins Nash - 1846-1928, age 82 yrs., Signal Corps.
    CSA.
Blanch Place Nash - Mar. 1910, age 60 yrs.
Jennie Nash - age 15 mos.

LOT 387
Ave. 6, Old 68
*Owners - W. G. Hitchings, S/H - Sold to Minnie L. Barkley, Nov.
    19, 1936.*
William G. Hitchings - Aug. 13, 1893, age 67 yrs.
Letitia T. Hitchings - Dec. 17, 1907, age 76 yrs.
Ruth T. Davis - Mar. 2, 1909, age 49 yrs.

Minnie Pitt Barkley - Feb. 22, 1963.
Brown L. Barkley - Mar. 2, 1937, age 61 yrs., USMC Spanish
American War.

LOT 388
Ave. 7, Old 74
Owner - Margaret Pablo, S/H
James F. Pablo - Dec. 15, 1918, age 50 yrs.
Virginia W. Pablo - May 14, 1936, age 58 yrs.
Harvey Blankenship - Feb. 18, 1944, age 74 yrs.
H. S. W. Blankenship - stillborn, Mar. 7, 1891.
George W. Lee - stillborn, Oct. 7, 1891.
Tunstall - stillborn, May 1, 1902.
Joseph Pablo - Jan. 29, 1887, age 57 yrs.
Margaret A. Pablo - Jan. 6, 1919, age 72 yrs.
Myrtle P. Blankenship - Feb. 14, 1953, age 75 yrs.
Walter L. Pablo - July 17, 1864, died May 26, 1933, buried on
this lot (not noted in burial records).

LOT 389
Ave. 6, Old 67
Owner - R. C. Marshall
Sarah Elizabeth N. Marshall - Feb. 16, 1960 (vault).
Rev. M. B. Marshall - Jan. 9, 1946, age 62 yrs.
Susan Lewis Marshall - Apr. 26, 1870-May 1, 1945, age 75 yrs.
Robert Stribling Marshall - Jan. 12, 1969.
Madison Lewis Marshall - 1903-1903, age 2 days.
Bagby - stillborn of R. H. Bagby, Apr. 15, 1906.
De Butts - stillborn, Mar. 2, 1927.
Freda Darley Marshall - Jan. 8, 1914, age 5 yrs.
Rebecca Coke Marshall - Feb. 4, 1963.
Lt. Richard C. Marshall - died Apr. 5, 1914, age 69 yrs., 7th Va.
Calv. CSA.
Mary Catherine Wilson Marshall - July 31, 1891, age 47 yrs.
Myra St. J. Marshall - Nov. 19, 1881, age 15 yrs.
Kate W. Marshall - Jan. 29, 1875, reinterred Dec. 26, 1888, age
1 day.

LOT 390
Ave. 7, Old 75
Owner - Alexander B. Davis
Lerenna Davis - Jan. 2, 1942.
James A. Davis - Feb. 14, 1947, age 73 yrs.
Lillian R. Davis - Nov. 14, 1928, age 47 yrs.
Willie Ella Davis - Jan. 4, 1910, age 43 yrs.

Alexander Davis - Aug. 7, 1907, age 64 yrs.
Virginia C. Davis - Jan. 3, 1886, age 43 yrs.
Harry W. Davis - Corpl. Co. L, 2nd Va. Inf. Spanish American War.
Emmette Linwood Davis - Feb. 28, 1903, age 33 yrs.
Richey Davis - June 21, 1906, age 6 mos.
Louis B. Stevenson - Mar. 15, 1892, age 48 yrs.

LOT 390
Ave. 7, Old 76
Owner - J. B. Davis
1 grave - no name.
John B. Davis - Oct. 19, 1887, age 42 yrs.
Georgie L. Davis - Feb. 8, 1895, age 39 yrs.
John B. Davis - Oct. 30, 1961, age 83 yrs.
Mrs. Jane Davis Cason - Aug. 27, 1967 (vault).

LOT 391
Ave. 6, Old 66
Owner - Mrs. H. Almy, N/H
2 graves - no names.
Capt. Holer Almy - Sept. 25, 1887, age 57 yrs.
Frances A. Almy - June 18, 1922, age 89 yrs.
Ambrose B. Almy - age 1 yr. 22 days.
Julia M. Jenkins - removed from Section 8, reinterred Feb. 27, 189-, buried June 24, 1897, age 36 yrs.
A. D. Jenkins - July 6, 1900.
Walter A. Jenkins - May 27, 1912, age 27 yrs.
W. G. Armstrong - May 25, 1895, age 49 yrs.

LOT 392
Ave. 6, Old 66
Owner - Thomas Roberts, S/H
Grace R. Roberts - June 7, 1947, age 78 yrs.
C. C. R. - 1830-1887.
William Thomas Roberts - July 12, 1938, age 72 yrs.
Samuel Murphy - Feb. 14, 1946, age 52 yrs.
Grace Roberts Murphy - Sept. 11, 1974.
Mary Gillernand Milford - July 28, 1962, age 78 yrs.

LOT 393
Ave. 6, Old 65
Owner - W. L. Petit, N/H
Fannie L. P. Bartlett - Dec. 17, 1953, age 70 yrs.
Charles Albert Bartlett - 1874-1928, age 54 yrs.

Baby Boy Bartlett - Apr. 20, 1944.
Arthur A. Bartlett - Oct. 7, 1917, age 8 days.
T. E. Bland - Feb. 5, 1895, age 20 yrs. 10 mos.
Henry E. Petit - Sept. 25, 1888, age 1 yr. 11 mos.
W. L. Petit - Jan. 2, 1888, age 34 yrs.
Alice M. Petit - 1861-1933, age 71 yrs.

LOT 394
Ave. 6, Old 65
Owner - E. J. Houston, S/H
4 graves - no names (possibly E. J. and Cora Houston).
Mamie M. Houston - Dec. 10, 1922, age 21 yrs.
Conrad Horst - Feb. 6, 1905, age 47 yrs.
Cora A. Horst - July 12, 1891, age 1 yr., 2 mos.
Gracie E. Horst - June 12, 1888, age 5 yrs.
Marie Sue Horst - July 22, 1897, age 11 mos. 24 days.

LOT 395
Ave. 6, Old 64
Owner - A. J. Richardson, N/H
Aileen Richardson - Oct. 8, 1897, age 3 yrs. 4 mos.
Lillian Richardson - Nov. 10, 1959, age 85 yrs.
Andrew Richardson - Oct. 5, 1950, age 84 yrs.
Note: Not listed in plot book:
Andrew Junius Richardson, Jr. - 1887-1974 and Agnes, wife of
    Junius, Apr. 5, 1888, body donated to science.

LOT 396
Ave. 7, Old 77
Owners - James H. Boyd, E/H - W. J. Bidgood, W/H
W. M. James Bidgood - Feb. 9, 1950, age 78 yrs.
Mary Bidgood - July 25, 1954, age 72 yrs.
Sarah Nash Bidgood - Jan. 29, 1909, age 63 yrs.
William J. Bidgood - June 18, 1886, age 39 yrs.
James H. Boyd, July 29, 1905, age 44 yrs.
Fannie W. Boyd - Jan. 29, 1890, age 23 yrs.
Mamie Adelaide Boyd - Aug. 31, 1963.
Mrs. Delandy Curlin - Jan. 25, 1890, age 62 yrs.

LOT 397
Ave. 6, Old 64
Owner - W. L. Pablo, S/H
Walter L. Pablo - May 26, 1933, age 69 yrs.
Sallie May Pablo - Apr. 18, 1962, age 76 yrs.
Boyan - stillborn, Jan. 17, 1917.

LOT 398
Lot 20 x 30, Ave. 7
Owner - J. L. Hatton
Alexander Hatton - Dec. 25, 1891, age 61 yrs.
Susan Rebecca Hatton - Mar. 20, 1902, age 71 yrs.
Alexander Hatton, M.D. - 1869-1924, age 54 yrs.
Mattie A. Hatton - June 14, 1947, age 77 yrs.
Rev. James Chisholm - 1815-1855, First Pastor Saint Johns
    Church, Portsmouth, Va., died yellow fever.
Mrs. Jane Byrd Chisholm - 1823-1855.
Mary A. Hatton - Sept. 25, 1880, age 44 yrs.
Emmeline Hatton - Aug. 5, 1863, age 55 yrs.
John Goodrich Hatton - Oct. 9, 1860, age 54 yrs.
Mrs. Sarah B. Leckie - June 19, 1848.
Mrs. Ann H. Campbell - Jan. 11, 1841.
Elizabeth Riggs - Apr. 6, 1954, age 88 yrs.
Leckie Hatton - Sept. 22, 1950, age 77 yrs.
Edward Alexander Hatton III - 1898-1929, age 31 yrs.
Emmeline E. Hatton - June 12, 1861, age 9 mos.
Charles R. Hatton - Nov. 1, 1865, age 20 mos.
John S. Herbert - Dec. 16, 1886, age 61 yrs.
Octavia V. Herbert - Aug. 25, 1916, age 53 yrs.
Eleanor F. Hatton - Sept. 27, 1905, age 50 yrs.

LOT 399
Lot 20 x 22, Ave. 6, Old 147
Owners - Reed and Peed
Eliza Jane Jenkins - 1832-1899, age 67 yrs.
Miles Jenkins - Nov. 19, 1891, age 60 yrs., Va. Inf. CSA.
Eunice L. Jenkins - 1855-1931, age 76 yrs.
2 graves - no names.
William T. Reed - Aug. 26, 1909, age 83 yrs.
Susan Rebecca Gooding - June 28, 1909, age 59 yrs.
Carrie B. Peed - Dec. 29, 1899, age 24 yrs.
William D. Jenkins - May 27, 1935, age 24 yrs.
Leon Jenkins - Mar. 29, 1897, age 17 yrs. 10 mos.
John Reed Jenkins - Feb. 2, 1899, age 45 yrs. 6 mos.

LOT 400 - 402
Lot 22 x 34, Ave. 7, Old 139
Owner - William Moffatt Maupin
See Lot 202.
Georgianna Watts Holladay - Apr. 15, 1921, age 88 yrs.
James G. Holladay - Aug. 27, 1886, age 67 yrs.

Charles Owens - Mar. 19, 1886, age 53 yrs.
Anna M. Maupin - May 18, 1922, age 76 yrs.
Ellinor M. Watts - Nov. 13, 1883, age 7 yrs.
5 graves - no names.
E. M. Watts - June 11, 1890, age 55 yrs., CSA.
William Moffat, Sr. - Apr. 8, 1839.
Ann Moffat - June 27, 1834.
William Moffat, Jr. - Feb. 22, 1836, age 39 yrs.
Edward M. Watts - July 3, 1952, age 80 yrs.
Leigh Richmond Watts - Dec. 28, 1963, age 80 yrs.

LOT 401 - 403
Lot 20 x 22, Ave. 6, Old 146
Owner - George Watts, N / H
North Half:
No names (5).
South Half:
Sarah M Watts - 1838-1914, age 75 yrs.
Abraham S. Watts - 1832-1905, age 72 yrs., CSA.
Note: 1920, Harry Lee Watts, age 58 yrs., former member of
City Council, died King Daughters Hospital, Portsmouth, Va.,
after illness of three weeks, son of the late Judge A. S. Watts
and Mrs. Sarah Monronia Bain Watts.

LOT 404
Lot 20 x 34, Ave. 7, Old 138
Owner - Samuel Watts
Ann E. Watts - buried Mar. 12, 1894, age 79 yrs.
Riddick - stillborn of William Riddick.
Mrs. Martha Bacon - July 12, 1852.
S. W. Hunter - Va. Inf. CSA.
Mrs. Corani Ann Hunter - Nov. 13, 1877, age 63 yrs.
Eddie Hunter - Dec. 19, 1859, age 6 yrs. 11 mos.
Edna
E. R. Hunter - Nov. 9, 1884, age 63 yrs.
Louisa Ann Langley Watts - 1816-1902, age 86 yrs.
Samuel Watts - 1799-1878, age 79 yrs.
T. Benbury Hunter - June 16, 1873, age 37 yrs.
Virginia A. Hunter - Nov. 25, 1868, age 50 yrs.
Eliza Watts - July 23, 1861.
Margaret Langley Watts - 1846-1919, age 73 yrs.
Col. Winchester Watts - 1812-1857, age 45 yrs.
Col. Dempsy Watts - Aug. 12, 1841, age 68 yrs.
Mary Watts - May 29, 1835, age 57 yrs.
Dr. E. M. Watts - 1806-1849, age 42 yrs.

LOT 405 - 406
Lot 20 x 20, Ave. 6, Old 145
Owners - W. and T. C. Godwin
Virginia Godwin - May 22, 1884, age 69 yrs.
Sarah E. Williams - Aug. 27, 1884, age 56 yrs.
Charlie Jordan - Jan. 5, 1863, age 3 yrs.
Eliza F. Godwin Jordan - Dec. 21, 1862, age 26 yrs.
Frances A. Shackleford Godwin - Aug. 16, 1884, age 78 yrs.
Thomas C. Godwin - Apr. 3, 1839, age 30 yrs.
3 graves - no names.
Laura Brown - Jan. 3, 1918, age 71 yrs.
William Godwin - Oct. 18, 1890, age 60 yrs.

LOT 407
Lot 22 x 22, Ave. 6, Old 144
Owners - Tompkins and White
James Tompkins - 1799-1856, age 56 yrs.
Hattie L. White - 1858-1915, age 56 yrs.
John L. White - 1846-1926, age 79 yrs.
T. J. White - 9th Va. Inf. CSA.
Catherine, Mar. 1832, John H., Mar. 1837, and Caroline M.,
    Nov. 1834 - children of John and Mary White.

LOT 408
Lot 20 x 32, Ave. 7, Old 137
Owner - George M. Bain
James Gaskins Bain, 1820-1821, Mary Elizabeth Bain, 1822-
    1823, Martin Parks Bain, 1827-183- - children of Rev. George
    M. and Ann M. B. Bain.
Miss Sarah Tucker - 1819, age 84 yrs.
James Gaskins - 1827, age 66 yrs.
Mary Hurt Gaskins - 1851, age 88 yrs.
Miss Sarah Gaskins - 1862, age 73 yrs.
Ann M. B. Bain - June 29, 1863, age 61 yrs.
Rev. George M. Bain - June 6, 1874, age 76 yrs.
Jane Alice Bain - June 29, 1869, age 73 yrs.
James Britton Bain - 1822, age 50 yrs.
Dickey Bain - 1855, age 80 yrs.
Anna F. Bain - 1854, age 12 yrs.
Alice Bain - 1857, age 1 yr. 1 mo. 19 days.
Virginia White - 1859, age 2 yrs. 4 mos.
Margaret Lane - 1832, age 12 yrs.
N. A. White - 1852-1874, age 22 yrs., USN.
Jesse K. Bain - 1837, age 16 yrs.

Virginia A. White - 1829-1887, age 57 yrs.
Nathaniel Elisha White - 1827-1892, age 66 yrs.
George R. Atkinson, Jr. - 1849-1914, age 64 yrs.
Alice Forbes Atkinson - 1846-1922, age 75 yrs.
Note: Jan. 5, 1820 - Rev. George M. Bain married Ann M. B.
  Gaskins, surety - James Gaskins.

LOT 409
Lot 20 x 24, Ave. 6, Old 143
Owner - Robert Cutherell
Samuel D. Cutherell - died Feb. 12, 1912, age 54 yrs.
Father (no name) - died June 1840.
Mother (no name) - died Dec. 1847.
C. Cutherell - 9th Va. Inf. CSA.
L. Cutherell - 9th Va. Inf. CSA.
A. Cutherell - age 45 yrs., 3rd Va. Inf. CSA.
Robert D. Cutherell - died June 2, 1921, age 90 yrs.
Jennie S. Cutherell - died July 13, 1923, age 63 yrs.
W. H. Cutherell - buried Sept. 14, 1894, age 23 yrs.

LOT 410
Lot 20 x 30, Ave. 7, Old 136
Owner - Capt. James Jarvis
Mary Powell Jarvis - 1793-1858, age 65 yrs.
Elizabeth Jarvis Tee - 1856, age 76 yrs.
John Jarvis - Sept. 1860, age 45 yrs., USN.
Patsy Jarvis - 1795, age 8 yrs., buried Mathews County, Va.
Buried Trinity - names on monument.
John Jarvis, Sr. - 1754-1822.
John Jarvis, Jr. - 1832, age 46 yrs.
Ann Green Jarvis - 1757-1793, age 36 yrs.
Elizabeth Maclin Jarvis - 1809, age 81 yrs.
Nancy Jarvis - infant, 1793.
Louisiana Jarvis - Oct. 7, 1830, age 10 yrs.
Virginia Jarvis - 1823-1841, age 18 yrs.
Herbert Farant Loudon - 1856, age 37 yrs.
Missouri Jarvis Loudon - Nov. 23, 1856, age 27 yrs.
Capt. James Jarvis - 1791-1863, age 73 yrs.
Margaret Powell Pullin - mother of Mary Powell Jarvis, age 74
  yrs., 1849.
Margaret Ann Jarvis White - Oct. 25, 1859, age 42 yrs.
Ann D. Pullen Graves - age 36 yrs.
Elizabeth Jarvis Farant - Nov. 12, 1854, age 36, remains buried
  in Norfolk Co.
The following are grandchildren of James and Mary Powell

Jarvis as shown on the monument:

Louisana Farant - age 3 yrs. 6 mos.

George W. Farant - age 14 mos.

Sarah Farant - age 4 yrs., her remains with her mother in Norfolk.

Mary F. White - age 14 mos.

Mary Jarvis White - age 7 mos.

Martha W. White - age 2 yrs. 6 mos.

James Jarvis Loudon - age 15 mos.

St. John B. Aylon Loudon - age 12 months

Laura L. Loudon - age 7 yrs.

Mary R. Jarvis - age 16 days.

Mary V. Rives - buried June 29, 1889, age 43 yrs.

John Pullin - father of Mary Powell Jarvis, died 1828, age 65 yrs., remains buried under Court St. Baptist Church, Portsmouth, Va.

LOT 411

Lot 22 x 24, Ave 6., Old 142

Owner - W. H. Benthall

Fanny P. Thompson - Dec. 5, 1884, age 23 yrs.

Crawford Brooks - July 4, 1841, age 3 yrs.

Mrs. Sarah J. Parrish - Sept. 9, 1810, age 20 yrs.

Ester Ann Ferguson - Sept. 6, 1840, age 47 yrs.

Jane Alice Brooks - 1843-1918, age 75 yrs.

Mary E. Brooks - 1811-1900, age 88 yrs.

William Brooks - 1804-1884, age 80 yrs.

Mrs. Meriam Benthall - May 16, 1837, age 53 yrs.

Mrs. Frances D. Benthall - May 23, 1820, age 30 yrs.

Capt. William Benthall - 1780-1854, age 76 yrs.

Mrs. Margaret H. Jenkins - 1819-1851.

Jane Frances Niemeyer - 1816-1843.

1 grave - no name.

Note: Portsmouth News Paper - Apr. 5, 1918 - Died Wilmington, N.C., member Court St. Baptist, inter Cedar Grove. Pallbearers, Nephews: Charles B. Brooks, R. S. Brooks, F. T. Briggs, Griffin S. Brooks, James H. Brooks, and J. J. Bilisoly.

Jan. 18, 1900 - Mary E. Brooks, age 89, 317 Middle St., widow of the late William Brooks of Portsmouth, mother of: W. B. Brooks, Chief Engineer USN, retired of Erie, Pa.; Mrs. E. W. Manning of Wilmington, N.C.; E. C. Brooks, E. K. Brooks and C. F. Brooks all of Portsmouth; Mr. S. F. Brooks of War Dept. Washington, D.C.; Miss J. Alice Brooks of Portsmouth. Except for Mr. S. F. Brooks, who was called back to Washington, all of Mary E. Brooks' children were at her bedside during her last hours. She had been sick since Christmas. She was daughter of Capt. William Benthall, one of the largest landowners in Antibellum days. She was born Sept. 21, 1811, member Court St. Baptist Church for 60 years. There were 35 grandchildren at time of her death, over 100 direct descendants.

LOT 412
Lot 20 x 29, Ave 7
Owner - Henry Leslie
4 graves - no names.
John Foreman - July 1, 1950, age 82 yrs.
Elsie Foreman - Nov. 6, 1945, age 68 yrs.
Sarah L. Foreman - July 5, 1954, age 83 yrs.
Mrs. Sarah Ann Nash - 1810-1849, age 39 yrs.
Ann P. Leslie - Mar. 4, 1832, age 50 yrs.
Caroline Leslie Foreman - May 15, 1845, age 30 yrs.
Zachary Taylor Green - 1847-1906, age 58 yrs.
Florence Wonycott Green - 1853-1934, age 81 yrs.
Jane R. Green - Dec. 24, 1893, age 77 yrs.
Herbert Foreman - Oct. 1, 1910, age 16 yrs.

LOT 413
Lot 20 x 24, Ave. 6, Old 141
Owner - J. H. Jobson
Julett Mary Jobson - Jan. 24, 1925, age 82 yrs.
Alverda E. Jobson - Nov. 11, 1958, age 74 yrs.
Robert E. Jobson - Dec. 26, 1963, age 80 yrs.
Reserved for Beatrice E. Jobson.
Reserved for William L. Jobson.
3 graves - no names.
Capt. William A. Jobson - 1836-1915, age 79 yrs.
Minnie Lee Jobson - Dec. 28, 1950, age 73 yrs.
Jutson H. Jobson - Aug. 29, 1951, age 71 yrs.
George M. Jobson - Co. L, Va. Inf. Spanish American War.
Ellis B. Jobson - July 24, 1958, age 83 yrs.
Mary E. Jobson - 1830-1913, age 82 yrs.
Bessie Robinson Jobson - Feb. 21, 1935, age 50 yrs.
Mary M. White - Mar. 2, 1905, age 91 yrs.

LOT 414
Lot 20 x 28, Ave. 7, Old 134
Owner - William B. Bingley
1 grave - no name.
Mary Ann Bingley - July 7, 1926, age 103 yrs.

Edward Bingley - age 16 yrs.
Margaret L. Bingley - Feb. 2, 1896, age 56 yrs.
Sophia H. Bingley - 1798-1892, age 93 yrs.
William B. Bingley - 1797-1871, age 74 yrs.
Sophia B. Bingley - Sept. 2, 1855, age 19 yrs. 11 mos.
Sgt. William Bingley - died Mar. 3, 1865, Signal Corp. CSA.
Robert S. McMurran - buried Sept. 21, 1892, age 56 yrs.
James E. Wilson - buried Dec. 16, 1883, age 36 yrs.

LOT 415
Lot 20 x 24, Ave. 6, Old F1
Owner - W. V. H. Williams
John Williams - 1807-1888, age 80 yrs.
Mary Elizabeth Williams - Feb. 5, 1850, age 13 yrs.
Elizabeth Herbert - 1795-1864, age 69 yrs.
8 graves - no names.
John Luke Herbert - 1828-1886, age 58 yrs., 16th Va. Inf. CSA.
William V. Herbert - May 8, 1851, age 23 yrs.
Eliza J. White - Sept. 4, 1855, age 33 yrs.
Lillian Forrest F. Williams - Jan. 5, 1966.
William V. H. Williams, Jr. - Apr. 8, 1971 (vault).
Pauline Kearn Williams - June 9, 1966.
Miss Cecile Williams - Mar. 18, 1978 (vault).
Lucy Jane Williams - July 30, 1855, age 19 yrs.
Pauline L. Williams - 1817-1866, age 48 yrs.
Elizabeth G. Herbert - 1790-1862, age 72 yrs.
Sallie V. Williams - Oct. 25, 1924, age 64 yrs.
W. V. H. Williams - July 14, 1898, age 52 yrs.

LOT 416
Lot 20 x 28, Ave. 7, Old G
Owner - W. B. Lawrence
Mary Windle Seaward - May 10, 1860, age 81 yrs.
Elizabeth B. Carson Lawrence - Dec. 10, 1873, age 73 yrs.
Mary A. Seaward Lawrence - Oct. 24, 1847, age 24 yrs.
Henrietta S. Sherwood Lawrence - Feb. 24, 1886, age 80 yrs.
Sarah Turner Thomas - Sept. 18, 1906, age 70 yrs.
Daniel James Turner, Jr. - 1844-1914, age 70 yrs., Signal Corp.
    AN CSA.
Mary Lawrence Turner - July 16, 1938, age 92 yrs. 7 mos.
Ernest Turner - Dec. 21, 1952, age 81 yrs.
Jennie Turner - Oct. 29, 1950, age 72 yrs.
Ruth Leaward Turner - Dec. 18, 1962.
Mary Camp Turner - Oct. 1970 (vault).

LOT 417
Lot 20 x 22, Ave. 6, Old U1
Owner - James Brown, Jr.
1 grave - no name.
Francis Talbot Brown - 1832-1894, age 61 yrs.
James W. Brown - 1830-1896, age 66 yrs., Sgt. 9th Va. Inf. CSA.
Ebbieline B. Maupin - 1874-1928, age 53 yrs.
C. Owens - 9th Va. Inf. CSA.
James Brown Maupin - 1879-1910, age 32 yrs.
Ebbieline Brown Maupin - 1851-1899, age 49 yrs.
Edward Watts Maupin - 1848-1907, age 59 yrs.

LOT 418
Lot 20 x 29, Ave. 7, Old V1
Owner - George L. Neville
Sallie N. Neville - 1868-1905, age 37 yrs.
George L. Neville - 1836-1903, age 67 yrs.
Sarah E. Newman Neville - 1838-1910, age 72 yrs.
George L. Neville, Jr. - 1878-1906, age 28 yrs.
Neville - child, Sept. 28, 1955.
Nellie Neville - July 25, 1941, age 75 yrs.
Joseph H. Neville - Sept. 26, 1955, age 74 yrs.
Edith Margaret Neville - Feb. 25, 1945, age 66 yrs.

LOT 420
Lot 25 x 20, Ave. 7, Old V2
Owner - Mrs. Harriet Veale
Virginius B. Murden - Oct. 5, 1938, age 79 yrs. 10 mos.
Kate Dearborn Veale Murden - Dec. 22, 1938, age 81 yrs. 10
 mos.
Dorothy Veale Murden - Jan. 12, 1978.
Mary Abigail Veale Brinkley - 1854-1927, age 72 yrs.
Henry Allen Brinkley, 1848-1925, age 77 yrs.
Hallie V. Veale - Dec. 7, 1944, age 80 yrs.
Annie Garland Veale - Feb. 25, 1943, age 68 yrs.
Margaret Selena Veale - 1860-1931, age 71 yrs.
Simeon Veale - 1829-1903, age 74 yrs.
Harriett Avery Tee Veale - 1834-1921, age 86 yrs.
Murden - infant of D. B. and V. B. Murden, Jr., Oct. 13, 1932.

LOT 421
Lot 21 x 23, Ave. 6, Old C1
Owner - Dr. William Collins
Elizabeth Collins Hill - 1841-1926, age 84 yrs.
John Tompson Hill - 1839-1903, age 64 yrs., 6th Va. Inf. CSA.

Marion Hume Hill - Apr. 3, 1962, age 80 yrs.
Monument erected by Seaboard and Roanoke Railroad to Dr.
   William Collins.
Fannie G. Hill - Sept. 23, 1931, age 82 yrs.
Mary Elizabeth Chandler Hill - 1819-1893, age 74 yrs.
John Thompson Hill, Sr. - 1813-1842, age 28 yrs.
Elizabeth Gregory Hill - July 6, 1957, age 86 yrs.

LOT 422
Lot 26 x 18 1/2, Ave. 7, Old 206 1/2
Owner - Dr. William Collins
Fanny C. Hill - Jan. 21, 1958, age 84 yrs.
Collins Hill - June 18, 1971 (vault).
Evelyn Collins Hill - Nov. 26, 1965.
Blanche B. Hill - Dec. 11, 1949, age 79 yrs.
William Collins Hill - 1868-1934, age 65 yrs., Lt. Co. A, 4th Va.
   Volunteers, Inf. Spanish American War.
Mary Chandler Hill - Nov. 4, 1947, age 78 yrs.

LOT 423
Lot 22 x 23, Ave. 7, Old D1
Owner - Dr. William Collins
Frances Elizabeth Gregory Collins - 1819-1903, age 84 yrs.
Jennie Tucker Collins - 1851-1918, age 86 yrs.
C. W. Hill - died Aug. 12, 1896, age 55 yrs., 6th Va. Inf. CSA.
Marion Hume Hill - died Apr. 30, 1913, age 2 yrs.
J. L. Collins - June 30, 1918, age 65 yrs.
William Collins, M.D. - Sept. 8, 1855, age 51 yrs.
Margaret B. Collins - May 20, 1886, age 52 yrs.
Mary G. Baker - Aug. 24, 1890, age 7 yrs. 12 mos.

LOT 424
Lot 20 x 24, Ave. 7, Old 226
Owner - George R. Parrish
James Parrish - Nov. 22, 1941, age 3 mos.
Grace H. Parrish - June 12, 1979 (vault).
George Rose Parrish - Feb. 4, 1951, age 82 yrs.
Ola Coleman Parrish - Oct. 31, 1969 (vault).
James Parrish - Apr. 26, 1976.

LOT 425
Lot 20 x 22, Ave. 6, Old 126
Owner - D. J. Turner
George Patrick Porter - 1835-1903, age 68 yrs.
Sarah Sontag Porter - 1840-1906, age 66 yrs.

Martha Porter - Nov. 21, 1943, age 67 yrs.
Mary Porter - Feb. 6, 1945, age 79 yrs.
Ella Turney Bursley - 1847-1927, age 80 yrs.
Edward Webb - June 27, 1857.
Mrs. Sarah C. Turner - Oct. 9, 1857, age 40 yrs.
Daniel James Turner, Sr. - Dec. 30, 1890, age 78 yrs.
Edward Howard Turner - Mar. 24, 1909, age 57 yrs.
John Albert Turner - 1855-1920, age 67 yrs.
Clara Porter - 1862-1865.
James Middleton Butt - 1862-1864.
Sarah Camp Butt - 1857-1861.
Ernest M. Turner - Aug. 5, 1861, age 12 yrs.
Edward Webb Turner - Sept. 29, 1845.
Martha Elenor Turner - Jan. 4, 1843.
William Daniel Turner - 7 mos. 26 days.

LOT 426
Lot 20 x 24, Ave. 7, Old 133
Owner - L. Newsome
Albert Sidney Porter - 1870-1932, age 62 yrs.
Lena Mae Porter - Dec. 11, 1947, age 74 yrs.
George Patrick Porter - May 3, 1968, age 62 yrs.
Joseph Connor Bussey - Dec. 6, 1900-June 5, 1982.
Sarah Porter Bussey - Mar. 5, 1982.
Susan Porter Hughes - Mar. 2, 1974.
Edwin Bird Hughes - 1874-1921, age 47 yrs.
Edward Howard Porter - 1879-1933, age 55 yrs.
Elvire Tolleth - Mar. 15, 1953, age 79 yrs.
William P. Tolleth - Apr. 29, 1951, age 87 yrs.

LOT 427
Lot 10 x 22, Ave. 6, Old 125
Owner - E. Thompson, N/H
Sarah A. Thompson - June 26, 1847, age 24 yrs.
Ann Eliza Thompson - 1825-1895, age 70 yrs.
Ebenezer Thompson - 1817-1912, age 94 yrs.
Ida Virginia Thompson - 1844-1922, age 77 yrs.
William Joseph Jobson - May 19, 1927, age 65 yrs.
Ellie W. Thompson - Aug. 1, 1931, age 63 yrs.

LOT 428
Lot 20 x 23, Ave. 7, Old 132
Owner - Theal V. Williams
Josephine Theal - Feb. 23, 1841, age 5 mos. 5 days.
Mrs. Ann Williams - 1812-1832, age 19 yrs.

LOT 429
Lot 10 x 22, Ave. 6, Old 125
Owner - W. B. Johnson, S/H
Robert E. Thompson - June 17, 1878, age 32 yrs.
Mary Ann Thompson - 1819-1900, age 81 yrs.
Robert A. J. Thompson - 1815-1885, age 70 yrs.
Robert Andrew Rew - Aug. 10, 1867, age 10 mos.
Maywood Lee Johnson - Apr. 16, 1878, age 7 yrs. 9 mos.
Annie R. Johnson - 1854-1922, age 68 yrs.
Mary Edna Johnson - 1849-1888, age 39 yrs.
William B. Johnson - 1841-1902, age 60 yrs., 6th Va. Inf. CSA.

LOT 430
Lot 20 x 23, Ave. 7, Old 131
Note: No record of original owner of this lot. July 27, 1966,
   transferred by city clerk to Lester L. Knight, Cynthia K.
   Cooks and Caroline Green. Lot in Oak Grove exchanged for
   Cedar Grove.
Lester L. Knight - Jan. 12, 1984.
Carol Knight - Aug. 24, 1983.

LOT 431
Lot 9 x 22, Ave. 6, Old 124
Owners - Deans and Brother
2 graves - no names.

LOT 432 - 434
Lot 20 x 23, Ave. 7, Old 130
Owner - T. Sheperd, S/H and N/H
Sid Virginia Porter - Oct. 13, 1896, age 48 yrs.
Margaret A. Porter - July 1, 1895, age 73 yrs.
Joseph Fletcher Porter - Aug. 29, 1907, age 5 mos.
T. Sheperd
Aaron Porter - age 46 yrs., Co. L, 4th Va. Inf. Spanish American
   War.
2 graves - no names.
Milton H. Porter - Co. L, 4th Va. Inf. Spanish American War.
Mary Frances Porter - July 2, 1886, age 47 yrs.
Sarah Mildred Porter - Jan. 31, 1911, age 2 yrs.
Mary Elizabeth Porter - July 24, 1906, age 7 mos.

LOT 433
Lot 11 x 22, Ave. 6, Old 124
Owner - Deans and Brothers, S/H
Fannie R. Virnelson - 1843-1887, age 42 yrs.

Fannie Deans - 1814-1891, age 71 yrs.
Thomas D. Deans - 1809-1865, age 56 yrs.
2 graves - no names.
Fannie D. Virnelson - 1867-1871, age 11 yrs.
Emalia M. Virnelson - 1866-1878, age 12 yrs.

LOT 435
Lot 20 x 22, Ave. 6, Old 123
Owner - Mrs. J. Collins
Josaphine C. Collins - Jan. 10, 1929, age 66 yrs.
Collins - infant, June 9, 1911.
Infant of R. E. Johnson - Oct. 5, 1906, age 17 days.
3 graves - no names.
William James Moore - Nov. 25 1885, age 55 yrs.
Annie Moore - Sept. 2, 1893, age 73 yrs.
Julia Ann Moore - Apr. 16, 1899, age 98 yrs.

LOT 436 - 438
Lot 20 x 22, Old 129
Owners - Reed, USN, and Ellen C. Reed, S/H and N/H
South Half:
James L. Young - Jan. 1, 1897, age 34 yrs.
1 grave - no name.
North Half:
Miss Clara Ellen Reed - 1834-1891, age 57 yrs.
Miss Vernona Stratton Reed - 1845-1890, age 45 yrs.
Samuel Cameron Anderson - Aug. 3, 1848, age 9 yrs. 9 mos.
Paul E. Thomas - Mar. 31, 1899, age 4 mos.
Dr. Hope's child - Feb. 9, 1885.

LOT 437
Lot 20 x 22, Ave. 6, Old 122
Owner - William R. Whidbee
Henry Lee Perkins - Dec. 31, 1888, age 65 yrs.
Virginia B. Perkins - Feb. 8, 1897, age 61 yrs.
James W. Eastwood
6 graves - no names.
Susan M. Webb - 1840-1810, age 70 yrs.
William R. Whidbee - Nov. 12, 1873, age 80 yrs.
Diana Whidbee - June 26, 1868, age 67 yrs.
John M. Perkins - Dec. 20, 1908, age 40 yrs.
Mary V. Perkins - Sept. 19, 189-, age 31 yrs.
Carrie Lee Perkins - Mar. 10, 1920, age 46 yrs. 11 mos.

LOT 439
Lot 10 x 22, Ave. 6, Old 121
Owner - C. A. Myers, N/H
Mary Myers - Jan. 2, 1896, age 64 yrs.
Lt. Whitehurst - 3rd Va. Inf. CSA.

LOT 440
Lot 20 x 22, Ave. 7, Old 128
Owners - Grant and Thomas
Emma Coker Thomas - 1860-1923, age 63 yrs.
John William Wilson - Jan. 23, 1844, age 27 yrs.
Albert H. Grant - 1844-1900, age 54 yrs.
Minnie Lee Alexander - 1905-1928, age 23 yrs.
Jane Alice Thomas - Sept. 10, 1855, age 20 mos. 5 days.
Virginia Elizabeth Grant - 1892-1899, age 7 yrs. 3 mos.
Margaret E. Thomas - Sept. 11, 1855, age 28 yrs.
Jane A. Thomas - May 20, 1892, age 64 yrs.
Fred Grant, Jr. - stillborn, Jan. 1916.
Charles E. Grant - 1846-1899, age 52 yrs.
Mary Ann Grant - Aug. 16, 1879, age 65 yrs.
E. Madison Grant - May 28, 1890, age 77 yrs.
Children of Charles E. and Martha S. Grant:
  1. Geneva M. Grant - 1874-1876.
  2. John M. Grant - 1876-1876.
  3. Charles E. B. Grant - 1876-1881.
  4. Morris M. Grant - 1890-1891, age 1 yr. 5 mos.

LOT 441
Lot 10 x 22, Ave. 6, Old 121
Owner - Moses Taylor, S/H
William C. Taylor - July 18, 1904, age 70 yrs.
Emily Taylor Brounley - Feb. 15, 1927, age 86 yrs.
Mary D. Taylor - Sept. 23, 1855, age 59 yrs.
Moses Taylor
1 grave - no name.
George Taylor - 1837-1855, age 18 yrs.
James W. Brounley - 1835-1920, age 85 yrs.

LOT 442
Lot 21 x 17, Ave. 7, Old 127
Owner - Douglas
Josiah Fentress - July 9, 1850, age 39 yrs.
3 graves - no names.

LOT 443 - 444
Lot 20 x 22, Ave. 6, Old 120
Owner - James P. Oellers, S/H and N/H
Joseph B. Deans - Feb. 5, 1905.
Joseph L. Oeller - Mar. 21, 1859, age 25 yrs. 10 mos.
2 graves - no names.
The rest - no information.

LOT 445
Ave. 6, Old 119
Owner - McKewan
Susan F. Pery - Aug. 24, 1841, age 2 yrs.
Mary Frances Smith - Aug. 4, 1841, age 2 yrs. 4 mos.
Victoria Augusta Smith - Nov. 20, 1839, age 1 yr. 10 mos. 2 days.

LOT 446
Ave. 7, Old 86
Owner - W. T. Pearson
Margaret Pearson Cherry - May 29, 1887, age 2 yrs.
Mary Josephine Cherry - June 17, 1900, age 1 yr. 8 mos.
Lauferlette Harvey Pearson - Nov. 7, 1926 age 67 yrs.
Margaret S. Pearson - June 9, 1883, age 53 yrs.
Alice E. Pearson - age 11 mos.
William T. Pearson, Sr. - May 1, 1886, age 58 yrs.
William T. Pearson, Jr. - Aug. 3, 1892, age 36 yrs.

LOT 447
Ave. 7, Old 85
Owners - W. Talley, N/H - W. H. Elliott, S/H
North Half:
Theodore K. Tabb - Dec. 19, 1882, age 30 yrs.
Margaret Gayle Talley - June 30, 1965.
William I. Talley - June 30, 1956, age 78 yrs.
Kitty Garland Gayle - Apr. 24, 1885, age 73 yrs.
L. G. Gayle - Dec. 2, 1886, age 53 yrs., Sgt. 9th Va. Inf. CSA.
Mary Ann Hall - June 2, 1884, age 64 yrs.
Ann Elizabeth Elliott - Dec. 6, 1917, age 75 yrs.
Jennie Alma Butters McLean - June 12, 1889, age 27 yrs.
1 grave - no name.
William H. Elliott - Feb. 19, 1925, age 83 yrs.
Laura W. Hall - Nov. 22, 1922, age 70 yrs.

LOT 448
Ave. 7, Old 84

Owner - J. W. Ashton
J. W. Ashton - 1873-1881, age 8 yrs.
Elizabeth Cole Ashton - 1850-1922, age 72 yrs.
J. Whitcomb Ashton - 1836-1921, age 84 yrs., CSA.
Elizabeth Ashton - Apr. 2, 1951, age 75 yrs.
John N. Ashton - Apr. 15, 1944, age 63 yrs.
Edgar Ashton - 1839-1882, age 42 yrs., CSA.
Mary Ashton - 1813-1892, age 78 yrs.
Mrs. Willie A. Williams - Dec. 12, 1968 (cremation).
Charles T. Williams - 1874-1933, age 58 yrs.

LOT 449
Ave. 7, Old 83
Owner - G. F. Calvert, N/H
William G. Calvert - Feb. 19, 1958, age 75 yrs.
Carrie V. Calvert - June 5, 1925, age 72 yrs.
George F. Calvert - Nov. 22, 1936, age 83 yrs.
Frederick M. Calvert - July 19, 1970 (vault).
2 graves - no names.
Susan F. Calvert - June 23, 189-, age 14 yrs. 8 mos.
H. Calvert - Aug. 25, 189-, age 1 mo.
Annie Calvert - July 12, 1883, age 56 yrs.
Maggie Calvert - Apr. 5 188-, age 1 mo.
Carrie Calvert - Aug. 3, 1884, age 15 days.
Calvert - stillborn, May 13, 1890.
Ann Ella Calvert - Nov. 17, 1887, age 6 yrs. 2 mos.
Molly W. Calvert - Oct. 3, 1900, age 44 yrs.

LOT 450
Ave. 7, Old 83
*Owners - Mrs. D. Holland, S/H - Transferred to Mrs. E. H.
    Ayers, Mar. 1930.*
Dennis Edwin Holland - Oct. 11, 1882, age 37 yrs.
George Ann Holland - Mar. 17, 1929, age 79 yrs.
Eddine Holland - Feb. 11, 1904, age 25 yrs.
George W. Wilson - Nov. 30, 1897, age 1 yr. 3 mos.

LOT 451
Old 82
Owner - W. B. Carpenter, N/H
Frances A. Kenedy - died Dec. 23, 1899, age 44 yrs.
W. B. Carpenter - buried Dec. 8, 1894, age 49 yrs.
Ella C. Carpenter - died Jan. 24, 1936, age 72 yrs.
Gennieva Warren - died Mar. 29, 1919, age 33 yrs.

Cary J. Kennedy - age 16 yrs.
Alletia Sale - died Feb. 22, 1887, age 50 yrs.

LOT 452
Ave. 7, Old 82
Owner - M. G. Diggs, S/H
Jesse Earl Diggs - Feb. 27, 1907, age 34 yrs.
1 grave - no name.
Virginia T. Diggs - Apr. 28, 1898, age 49 yrs.
Lex Diggs - Apr. 30, 1892, age 49 yrs.
Larna F. H. L. - stillborn, Sept. 7, 1903.

LOT 453
Ave. 7, Old 79/80/81
Owners - B. W. Baker - Transferred to Barnabus W. Baker, Jan.
7, 1976.
Joseph Ball Baker
Allen G. Baker
Little Ida Baker - daughter of B. W. and Ida Baker.
Virginia Baker - Nov. 29, 1985 (vault).
Alberta Richardson Baker - Jan. 8, 1951.
Clarence Peed Baker - Nov. 12, 1944, age 62 yrs.
Barnabus William Baker - May 19, 1931, age 83 yrs.
Ida James Baker - June 14, 1931, age 78 yrs.
Emily Watts James - Jan. 23, 1894, age 63 yrs.
James Ball Baker - Mar. 27, 1929, age 2 mos.
Allen G. Baker - Jan. 29, 1889, age 1 yr.

LOT 453 B
Ave. 7, Old 79/80/81
Owners - Louisa Baker - Transferred to son, Barnabus Baker,
Jan. 7, 1976, 2 of 3 Lots.
Calvan A. Carney - Mar. 1, 1916, age 63 yrs.
Minnie C. Odeon Carney - Aug. 2, 1913.
William J. Odeon - Aug. 14, 1888, age 49 yrs.
Louisa Baker - Jan. 4, 1903, age 90 yrs.
Barnabus Baker - Aug. 13, 1877, age 71 yrs.
Adelaide C. Baker - Mar. 20, 1881, age 45 yrs.
1 grave - no name.
Monument
William Carney - Aug. 2, 1913, age 52 yrs.

LOT 453
Ave. 7, Old 79/80/81

Owners - H. A. Baker - Transferred to son, Barnabus W. Baker,
Jan. 7, 1976, 3 of 3 Lots.
Henry A. Baker - Nov. 28, 1930, age 88 yrs.
Kate Jourden Baker - Mar. 19, 1910, age 58 yrs.
Cecil M. Baker - Sept. 5, 1885, age 1 yr.
James Henry Baker - June 12, 1910, age 6 mos.
8 graves - no names.
Ethel Lee Fletcher Baker - Dec. 20, 1971 (vault).
Edwin Leroy Baker, Sr. - Jan. 23, 1974.
Hettie W. Odeon - Dec. 3, 1912, age 81 yrs.
L. Louise Odeon - June 18, 1904, age 49 yrs.
Infant Frank Odeon - stillborn, Mar. 6 189-.
William Carney - July 8, 1885, age 1 yr.
Gertrude Kaufman - Mar. 22, 1885, age 3 yrs.

LOT 454
Ave. 7, Old 78
Owner - George L. Foreman
Lydia W. Foreman - Nov. 10, 1907, age 80 yrs.
John A. Foreman - May 8, 1893, age 81 yrs.
Jennie Foreman - Nov. 25, 1943, age 93 yrs.
George L. Foreman - May 18, 1925, age 80 yrs.
William N. Foreman - May 18, 1925, age 80 yrs.
William N. Foreman - Nov. 18, 1900, age 61 yrs., 9th Va. Inf.
   CSA.
Mary W. Foreman - 1854-1934, age 80 yrs.
Lydia W. Foreman - Aug. 29, 1937, age 68 yrs.
Maggie Foreman - Sept. 29, 1949, age 94 yrs.

LOT 455
Ave. 7 East Wall, Old 78
Owner - E. Oakley Wood
Martha A. Wood - July 29, 1971 (vault).
Ernest Oakley Wood - Feb. 2, 1981 (vault).

ADAMS, 9 45 104 112
ADAMSON, 7
AINSWORTH, 96
ALEXANDER, 130
ALFRED, 111
ALGER, 114
ALLCAMP, 55
ALLEN, 69 81 113
ALLMOND, 105 106
ALMY, 116
ANDERSON, 55 60 73 129
ANDERTON, 3 56
APPENZELLER, 13
ARMISTEAD, 20-22 29 39 48 49
   52 67 94 100
ARMSTRONG, 6 116
ARRINGTON, 114
ASHTON, 38 77 132
ASSERSON, 13
ATKINSON, 21 121
AYERS, 132
AYLWIN, 85
BACON, 119
BAGBY, 115
BAGGETT, 40
BAGLEY, 6 70
BAGWELL, 103
BAIN, 3 4 17 18 38 48 100 101
   120 121
BAIRD, 107 108
BAKER, 21 104 126 133 134
BALL, 2 18
BALLENTINE, 2 16 17
BAORT, 109

BARKLEY, 114 115
BARLOW, 7 15 16 35
BARNARD, 18 30 67
BARNES, 53
BARNETT, 30
BARRETT, 14 54 88
BARRON, 111
BARTEE, 11
BARTLETT, 116 117
BAUGH, 62
BAUGHAM, 42
BAYTON, 49 64
BEACH, 112
BEATON, 110 113 114
BEAZLEY, 49
BELL, 89
BENSON, 15 20 107
BENTHALL, 80 122 123
BERKLEY, 81
BERNARD, 62
BETZEL, 12
BETZILL, 12
BIDGOOD, 78 80 117
BILISOLY, 6 7 19 21 29 30 48 83
   91 100 122
BINDERWALD, 45
BINFORD, 64
BINGHAM, 33
BINGLEY, 123 124
BISHOP, 47 48
BLACKNALL, 99 100
BLACKSTONE, 108
BLAMIRE, 29 110
BLAND, 117

BLANKENSHIP, 115
BLOW, 9 99
BLOXOM, 89
BOCKRINGER, 6
BOGART, 45
BOGG, 35
BOGGS, 35
BORUM, 38 106 112
BOSWICK, 25
BOURKE, 6 7
BOUSH, 29 31 71
BOWERS, 75
BOYAN, 117
BOYD, 28 117
BOYKIN, 22
BRENNAN, 30
BRENT, 37
BREUOORTH, 71
BREWER, 45
BRICKHOUSE, 101
BRIDGES, 43
BRIGGS, 78 122
BRINKLEY, 5 11 125
BRITTINGHAM, 11 12
BROCKETT, 78
BRODRICK, 97
BROOKS, 78-80 84 107 109 122
BROUGHTON, 30
BROUNLEY, 59 112 130
BROWN, 10 11 28 29 79 80 93
    100 106 112 120 125
BROWNE, 59 69
BROWNLEY, 16 17
BRUCE, 102
BRYSON, 82
BUFF, 6 44
BULLOCK, 23
BURFORD, 9
BURGESS, 5
BURKE, 75
BURMESTER, 53
BURNS, 52
BURROUGHS, 30 31
BURSLEY, 127
BURTON, 26 68 69

BUSH, 67
BUSSEY, 127
BUTLER, 67
BUTT, 26 41 57 70 73 74 79 127
CABELL, 38
CALVERT, 42 132
CAMM, 19 49
CAMPBELL, 43 118
CAPPS, 63
CAREY, 7 30 31
CARNEY, 133 134
CARPENTER, 132
CARR, 32 84
CARROLL, 45
CARTER, 89
CASON, 59 116
CASSELL, 68 81 88-90
CHADWICK, 22
CHAMBERS, 92
CHANDLER, 98 106
CHAPMAN, 19 100 101
CHARLES, 108
CHERRY, 53 67 131
CHILD, 69
CHILES, 81
CHISHOLM, 118
CHOAT, 51
CHOATE, 49
CHOATES, 48
CITY, 85
CLARK, 36 43 55 56 102
CLARKE, 91
CLAYTON, 18
CLEAVES, 59
CLEMENTS, 79
COCKE, 90 91
CODD, 73
COLEMAN, 54
COLES, 91
COLLINS, 28 50 77 93 125 126
    129
COOK, 46
COOKE, 64 65 89 98
COOKS, 128
COOPER, 60

HICKMAN, 85 98 108
HIGGINBOTHAM, 16
HIGGINS, 102
HIGGS, 85
HILL, 10 19 98 103 106 125 126
HILTON, 8
HINGERTY, 23
HITCHINGS, 114
HOBDAY, 3 4 16 28 29 37
HODGES, 21 26 94 104 108
HOFFMAN, 86
HOLDEN, 58
HOLLADAY, 60 118
HOLLAND, 132
HOLSTEAD, 54
HOLT, 21 22
HOOPS, 28 29
HOPE, 50 54 97 112 129
HOPKINS, 5
HORST, 117
HORTON, 112
HOUSTON, 117
HOWELL, 57
HOWLAND, 60
HOWLETT, 40
HUDGINS, 3 16 33
HUESTIS, 101
HUGHES, 41 96 127
HUGWOD, 35
HUME, 14 19 101 102
HUMPHLETT, 57
HUMPHRIES, 54
HUNT, 86
HUNTER, 84 119
HURST, 52
HUTCHENS, 86
HUTCHINS, 95
HUTSON, 104
IRONMONGER, 88 94
IVY, 90
JACK, 102
JACKS, 100
JAMERSON, 57
JAMES, 4 86 133
JARVIS, 43 58 77 121 122

JENKINS, 72 99 116 118 122
JERNIGAN, 91
JOBSON, 16 67 68 123 127
JOHNSON, 21 25 29 41 47 74
   102 128 129
JOHNSTON, 1 12
JOILEY, 24
JOINER, 47
JONES, 47 68 73 74 93
JORDAN, 46 83 108 120
JOYCE, 106 107
JOYNER, 47
KANTZ, 41
KAUFMAN, 109 134
KEAN, 110
KEARNS, 58
KEELING, 26
KEENAN, 75
KELLUM, 72
KENEDY, 132
KENNEDY, 133
KILBY, 46
KING, 2 40 41 55 81 88 114
KIRBY, 9
KNAPP, 58
KNIGHT, 128
KNOTT, 109
LAMONS, 69
LAND, 44
LANDENBERGER, 5
LANE, 6 120
LANGHORNE, 29 33 34 81
LASH, 29 100 101 106
LATIMER, 22
LAUGHRIDGE, 82
LAURENCE, 7 12 36 37 54 56
LAWRENCE, 16 45 124
LAYLOR, 45
LECKIE, 118
LEE, 115
LEGRAND, 33
LEIGH, 71
LELSE, 19
LEMOSY, 112
LESLIE, 123

141

ROCHE, 47
RODGERS, 5 90
RODMAN, 103
ROGERS, 58 95 96
ROPER, 97
ROSE, 89
ROSER, 109
ROSS, 90 98
ROSSER, 106
ROUNTREE, 46
ROY, 38 42
ROYAL, 16
ROYALL, 41
RUDD, 69 89
RUSS, 25
RUSSELL, 42 58 96
RUTTER, 64
SADLER, 47
SALE, 133
SAVAGE, 21 27 103
SAWYER, 107
SCARFF, 26
SCHOOLEY, 112
SCHOOLFIELD, 55 71
SCHROADER, 104
SCHRODER, 20
SCHROEDER, 20 107
SCHULTE, 91
SCOTT, 76 94 99 111
SEAWARD, 124
SELWYN, 45
SEYMORE, 24
SHACKLOCK, 58
SHANE, 5 25
SHANNON, 2 27 71
SHAVER, 20
SHELTON, 5
SHEPERD, 128
SHEPPERD, 1
SHERWOOD, 4 78 80
SHULTZ, 80
SILVESTER, 10
SIMMONDS, 79
SIMMONS, 23 36 58
SIMPSON, 97

SINGLETON, 68
SIRIAN, 85 86
SKEETER, 20 42
SKINNER, 65
SMALL, 54
SMITH, 12 13 15 17 24 37 41 42
    54 60 68 76 90 114 131
SNEED, 46
SNYDER, 51 52
SPARROW, 50
SPAULDING-MURDOCK, 40
SPENCER, 89
SPIVEY, 54
SPOONER, 80 89
SPRATLEY, 90 91
SPRING, 42 94
STANLEY, 39
STANWOOD, 27 50
STAPLES, 23 24 35 104 105
STEARN, 46
STEVENS, 52 53
STEVENSON, 116
STEWART, 41 78
STILES, 90
STOAKES, 5 6 109
STOKES, 31 95 96
STORY, 37
STOUT, 35 36
STRATTON, 5 105
STRINGER, 96
STROUD, 16
STUBBS, 41
STURTEVANT, 28
SULLEN, 99
SUMMERS, 82
SWANN, 29
SWEPSON, 25
SYKES, 50
TABB, 23 49 104 131
TALBOT, 62 63
TALLEY, 131
TALLMAN, 99
TART, 56
TATEM, 40 43
TAYLOR, 14 24 35 41 42 44 45 60

www.ingramcontent.com/pod-product-compliance
Lightning Source LLC
Chambersburg PA
CBHW072152270326
41930CB00011B/2398